Foundations
of
Trading

Foundations of Trading

Developing Profitable
Trading Systems
using
Scientific Techniques

Howard B. Bandy

Blue Owl Press, Inc.

ISBN-13: 978-097918386-7
LCCN: 2016912301

Published by
Blue Owl Press
3220 Crescent Avenue, #65
Eugene, OR 97408

Published 2016
Printed in the United States
19 18 17 16   1 2 3 4 5 6 7 8 9 10

Disclaimer

This book is an educational document. Nothing in this book is intended as, nor should it be construed to be, investment advice.

The views expressed herein are the personal views of Dr. Howard B. Bandy. Neither the author nor the publisher, Blue Owl Press, Inc., have any commercial interest in any of the products mentioned. All of the products described were purchased by the author at regular retail prices.

Investing and trading is risky and can result in loss of principal. Neither this book in its entirety, nor any portion thereof, nor any follow-on discussion or correspondence related to this book, is intended to be a recommendation to invest or trade mutual funds, stocks, commodities, options, or any other financial instrument. Neither the author nor the publisher will accept any responsibility for losses which might result from applications of the ideas expressed in the book or from techniques or trading systems described in the book.

All results shown are from simulations. None are the results from actual trades. Neither past actual performance, nor simulations of performance, assure similar future results, or even profitable future results.

Programs

The programs used as examples have been tested and are believed to be correct. However, errors may still remain. Programs are "as is" and without support beyond correction of errors. It is the reader's responsibility to verify the accuracy and correctness of all programs before using them to trade. Results will depend on the specific data series used, and will vary with changes in settings such commission, slippage, and delay between signal and transaction.

Programs have been written for clarity and educational value. Computational efficiency is not a consideration. Each and every method, technique, and program has many possible options and alternative implementations. No effort has been made to consider all of them, or to provide computer code to anticipate or accommodate them.

In an effort to maintain ease of understanding the basic concepts illustrated by the programs, code for detecting and gracefully handling run-time errors has been omitted.

Algorithms and programs are not guaranteed to be either without error or suitable for use. Do careful and complete testing and validation of all methods, techniques, and programs on your own computer using your own data before using any in live trading.

Errata

If you find an error, please report it in an e-mail to:
    support@BlueOwlPress.com

Corrections will be posted to the errata file:
    http://www.FoundationsOfTrading.com/Errata.html

Questions, comments, discussion

Post questions and comments, share ideas and results, and participate in a discussion of concepts and techniques at the Blue Owl Press blog site:
    http://www.BlueOwlPress.com/WordPress/

Contents

Chapter 1 — Introduction

This book is about developing trading systems using scientific techniques. It applies to any of the commonly traded financial issues—stocks, bonds, mutual funds, exchange traded funds, futures, currencies, FOREX, commodities. The systems are based on analysis of the price and volume of previous transactions made in open markets.

As the subtitle says, this book describes the importance of using the scientific method, and its derivatives related to engineering design and data science, in the process of developing trading systems and trading management systems.

The purpose of this book is to outline a few basic and relatively simple, but not necessarily simplistic, ideas that will assist readers in their system trading. The focus is developing and managing systems that have a good trade-off between reward and risk, and systems in which the trader will have confidence. And to draw attention to some common misconceptions related to trading system development and trading that can easily lead to systems that are likely to be difficult to trade confidently, riskier than expected, and less profitable than expected.

The process is quantitative, data driven, evidence based, and statistically sound. The resulting systems are rule based, monitored daily, and managed to hold risk to a level that is in keeping with the trader's risk tolerance.

This book is not intended to be encyclopedic. It lays out the foundations and their justifications. There is little computer code in this book. Implementation details, including fully disclosed examples, can be found in my other materials. See the Bibliography.

As every engineer will tell you, in order to design and develop a product, you must know how it will be used; in order to design and develop a process, you must know how it will be measured and managed.

Our product will be a profitable trading system. Our process will be designing and verifying the system, then monitoring its performance and determining the maximum safe position size. Our metrics will be account growth, normalized for risk.

Goal

There is a goal common to all traders:

> To have confidence that the signals generated by the trading system precede trades that provide rewards adequate to compensate for the risk.

> The key word is confidence.

> The primary limitation is risk.

The remainder of this book explains how to best achieve that goal using rigorous and statistically sound quantitative technical analysis with well defined rules generated from analysis of the price data developed using principles of the scientific method and its related techniques.

Major Changes

Some major changes are taking place in trading system development and trading management. Each of these phrases identifies the "from" and the "to."

Broadly—Galileo to Hubble   Frequentist to Bayesian

Charts to Equations   Idea driven to Data driven

Subjective to Objective   Profit oriented to Risk oriented

TSDP* to Machine learning   Deterministic to Probabilistic

Indicators to Patterns   Reaction to Prediction

Stationary to Dynamic   Decision tree to Non-linear

Position size into Trading mgmt   p-value to Confusion matrix

Single backtest to Monte Carlo   Equity curve to Distribution

Impulse signals to State signals

Trade-by-trade accounting to marked-to-market daily

* TSDP: Traditional Trading System Development Platform

Decisions and Uncertainty

Most of the decisions we make in life are choices that involve weighing opportunity against risk. Most of the calculations are extremely complex and involve estimating costs and values of things not easily quantified—whom to choose as a partner, where to live, what employment to pursue. All are specific applications of making decisions under uncertain conditions. It seems that the more important the decision, the less opportunity we have to practice and the more important it is to be correct early in the process.

How we handle our finances is certainly an important area, and one where we don't get many practice runs. For traders, the goal is maximizing trading profits while minimizing the risk of bankruptcy. In the spectrum of life's activities, this is a problem that is relatively easy to quantify and analyze. The major aspects already have easily measured units of value—dollars. And, given a little understanding of probability and statistics, along with some computer data analysis, we can outline a plan.

Trading and Investing

By trading I mean buying and selling financial instruments with the intention of increasing wealth. While the terms are often used interchangeably, I distinguish between trading and investing.

An investment is a use of funds to acquire some asset, often a tangible asset such as real estate, that will not be sold during the investor's lifetime. The details of the transaction and directions for inheritance are recorded in the investor's will.

A trade is a use of funds to acquire some asset that will be sold at some point in the trader's lifetime. In the context of this book, trading is buying and selling financial instruments—stocks, bonds, mutual funds, exchange traded funds, futures contracts, currency contracts—with fairly short holding periods.

There is a third category—expense. When funds are spent, or the item purchased is consumed or becomes worthless, the transaction is an expense. There is no residual value.

Transactions sometimes change categories.
- Stock or real estate may be purchased with the intention of holding forever and passing it on to heirs, but sold for any number of reasons.
- A stock may be purchased in anticipation of a rise in its price and sale for a profit, only to have its price drop to a very low level, so the trader turns the trade into an investment by holding the stock indefinitely hoping for a recovery.
- An automobile may be purchased expecting it to become a classic and collector's item—later to become damaged and a total loss.

A person who buys a stock with the expectation of selling it at a profit is a trader, regardless of what he thinks at the time of the purchase. I believe that almost everyone who owns stocks, bonds, mutual funds—even real estate—initially intending to hold indefinitely is a trader; just one who has not yet planned the exit from his position.

With the exception of an investment made with the explicit intention of passing it on to heirs, all positions will eventually be closed out. Even investments made during prime working years which are intended to fund expenses in the far future, such as retirement, will eventually be sold.

Technical Analysis and Fundamental Analysis

There are two broad categories of financial data—technical data and fundamental data. Correspondingly, there are two broad techniques for determining which issues to select and when to buy and sell—technical analysis and fundamental analysis.

Technical data consists of the price and volume of transactions freely made, recorded, and published. *Technical analysis* examines price and volume data hoping to detect patterns that precede profitable trading opportunities.

Fundamental data consists of government economic reports, corporate management reports, and analyst estimates of future economic and business activity. *Fundamental analysis* examines economic series and corporate data hoping to identify companies whose share price will increase and economic conditions favorable to holding stocks.

Efficient Market Hypothesis

The efficient market hypothesis holds that asset prices fully and immediately reflect all information about the asset. The degree of efficiency is described as being one of three forms:

- Strong form. All information about a company—public and confidential—is reflected in the share price of the company. There is no data that provides a trader, investor, or even an insider an opportunity to profit from further analysis of the data.
- Semi-strong form. All public information is reflected in the share price. Insiders may have knowledge that gives them an advantage.
- Weak form. The current price of a stock incorporates the historical prices. No analysis of price history provides a trader an opportunity to profit.

There is a large body of discussion devoted to whether the financial markets are efficient or inefficient. Efficiency, in this context, refers to the question of whether variations in prices are just random noise, or whether they represent potentially profitable trading opportunities, and what categories of information are valuable to a trader.

Those favoring the point of view that markets are *strongly* efficient say that even insider information is already reflected in the price of the stock and is not valuable enough to create profitable trades. The capital asset pricing model and mean-variance portfolio construction follow from strongly efficient views.

Those favoring the point of view that markets are *semi-strongly* efficient say that public information, including both fundamental information and historical price information, is already priced into the market and cannot be used to make profitable trades.

Those favoring the point of view that markets are *weakly* efficient say that historical price and volume information is not valuable enough to create profitable trades.

Clearly, insiders do very well trading on information that only they have, so the markets are not strongly efficient. And there is enough controversy about the validity of any form of the efficient market hypothesis that all three forms may be disproved. In order for quantitative trading systems of the type this book discusses to be profitable, the market must have some inefficiency. If there are not persistent patterns and trends that we can identify and trade profitably, then we are all wasting our time.

Warren Buffett of Berkshire Hathaway is reported to have said, "I'd be a bum in the street with a tin cup if the markets were always efficient.[1]"

David Harding of Winton Capital Management asks "Efficient Market Theory—When Will it Die?[2]"

Fundamental Analysis

I am among those who feel that fundamental data provides no information from which a trader can profit. Fundamental analysis is based on the premise that a stock, bond, fund, commodity, or a market as a whole, has an underlying intrinsic value. By analysis of the fundamental characteristics, such as the assets, liabilities, income, supply, or demand, that value can be determined.

Fundamental data for a company includes earnings, sales, inventory turnovers, price to earnings ratios, price to sales ratios, dividend payout ratios, and any other information that might be reported on a balance sheet or income statement. Fundamental data extends to government and private research bureau reports, including gross domestic product, inflation, balance of payments, and any other data reported periodically. In general, fundamental data is only gathered, summarized, and reported—it does not represent trades.

Economists and security analysts who focus on fundamental information have developed mathematical models of the fair price for one share

---

1   Fortune, April 3, 1995
2   https://www.wintoncapital.com/getmedia/ccba88f6-a914-45d9-8b0d-fcf9db47644c/Efficient-Market-Theory-when-will-it-die.pdf

of the stock—it is the current book value of the stock plus the present value of all future dividends that will be paid to that one share. Any difference between the actual price of the stock and this fundamental value of the stock represents an opinion on the part of shareholders.

The fundamental analyst uses data that is reported by a company or agency to create subjective models. She may use charts to gauge overall price activity, but with few mathematically defined indicators.

While fundamental analysis may have value in its own right, there are several problems associated with incorporating it into trading models. See Appendix A for more detail.

Technical Analysis

Technical analysis, whether from the most subjective chart analysis, through quantitative analysis, to the most sophisticated machine learning and statistical analysis, is based precisely on the assumption that there is information in the publicly available price history. The underlying assumptions of technical analysis are:

☆ The markets we model are sufficiently inefficient for us to make a profit trading them.

☆ There is information—*patterns*—in the historical price series that can be used to identify profitable trading opportunities.

☆ Trading systems can be designed to recognize the patterns and give buy and sell signals.

☆ Patterns similar to those found in the historical data will continue to be found in future data.

Technical analysis began as chart analysis, and has developed a large body of subjective interpretation of chart artifacts such as flags, retracements, head-and-shoulders, and trend lines, to name just a few. We traders are all very good at selective vision—we see what we want to see. We can look at a chart and see examples of a big gain following, say, the breakout of a triangle pattern. Daniel Kahneman describes this tendency in his excellent book *Thinking, Fast and Slow*[3]. Thinking we have found a good trade entry technique, we can define those conditions in very precise terms and have the unbiased computer search all the data for instances of that pattern. The results do indeed show a profit for the pattern we saw so clearly. Often it also shows losses from many similar patterns that we either did not see or chose not to acknowledge; and it sometimes shows signals that appear, and then disappear as additional data points are added to the chart.

Quantitative analysis refines technical analysis by:

• Removing the judgment associated with ambiguous chart patterns.

---

3   https://www.amazon.com/
    Thinking-Fast-Slow-Daniel-Kahneman/dp/0374533555/

- Defining unambiguous, mathematically precise indicators.
- Requiring an indicator value for every data bar.
- Requiring that no indicator or signal may change in response to data that is received after it has been initially computed.
- Making extensive use of mathematical models, numerical methods, and computer simulations.
- Applying statistical validation techniques to the resulting trading models.

Many Trading Techniques

There has been trading for thousands of years. Beginning with the earliest markets—food, wine, spices, gems, cloth—people have bought and sold. Not only for their own use or as raw materials for the products they make, but also with the intent of making a profit through the trades.

Deciding what to trade, when to buy, and when to sell has been, and continues to be, the trader's craft. Even before personal computers, traders monitored the price and size of trades, created charts with plots based on prices, and looked for indications that prices were likely to change.

Over the years, there have been many refinements—standard contracts, regulated exchanges, central clearing, low commissions, powerful and inexpensive personal computers, trading-specific software, and publications of trade data. The barriers to becoming a trader are quite low and the reward for being successful are quite high. It is no wonder that trading is an attractive activity.

Why Traders Stop Trading

Assume a trader has a method—mechanical or discretionary—that she has been using successfully. Also assume that she understands both herself and the business of trading, and wants to continue trading. Why would she stop trading that particular system?

Here are a few possibilities:
1. The results are too good.
2. The results are not worth the effort.
3. The results are not worth the stress.
4. She has enough money.
5. There is a serious drawdown

1. Results are too good

She is afraid that this cannot possibly continue.

Her system—any system—works when the logic of the model and the data it analyzes are synchronized. There are many reasons why systems fail and should be taken offline, but a sequence of winning trades should be seen as a success.

She should continue trading it until one of the other reasons to stop happens.

2. Results are not worth the effort

There is not much gain, but not much loss either. Other things in life are more important. On balance, the time, energy, and resources would be more productively applied doing something else.

3. Results are not worth the stress

Performance is satisfactory, but at a high cost—worry and loss of sleep. Regardless of the position size indicated by the metrics of risk, the positions being taken are too large.

She should either reduce position size or have someone else execute the trades.

4. She has enough money

Not matter how good a system is, there is always a risk of serious loss.

When she has reached her goal, she should retire from trading.

5. There is a serious drawdown

The magnitude of the drawdown needed for it to be classified as serious is subjective. Among my colleagues and clients, those who manage other people's money typically want drawdown limited to single digits. Those trading their own money may be willing to suffer drawdowns of 15 or 20 percent.

But there is a level at which everyone stops trading the system—preferably while the account still has a positive balance.

My view is that experiencing a large drawdown is the primary reason people stop trading a system.

What causes a large drawdown and how should the trader react to it?
- The system is broken.
- There was an unexpected sequence of losing trades.
- The system is out of sync.
- The position size is too high.

As the account balance drops from an equity high into a drawdown, it is not possible to determine which is The reason.

All of the reasons are true to some extent. A system that is broken breaks because the logic and the data become unsynchronized, causing an unexpected sequence of losing trades and at a time when position size was too high for conditions.

The solution is two-fold.
1. Continually monitor system performance and system health.
2. Modify position size to reflect recent performance.

During the trading system development process, a baseline of system performance is established. The out-of-sample trades from the walk forward phase are a good source of this data. Personal risk tolerance and system risk, taken together, determine position size for that system performance. As system performance changes, position size must also change.

Position size varies in response to system health.

Do not continue to trade a system that has entered a serious drawdown expecting that it will recover. It may recover on its own; it may require readjustment; or it may be permanently broken and never work again.

Take it offline and either observe it until recent paper-trade results demonstrate that it is healthy again, or send it back to development.

The correct position size for a system that is broken is zero.

The Scientific Method

The scientific method, in use since the work of Kepler and Galileo in the 17th century, is a process to learn general principles about some system through analysis of data and experimentation.

As Figure 1.1 illustrates, it consists of a sequence of steps, including:
• Observation and measurement of data.
• Hypothesis statement and model specification.
• Prediction and validation.

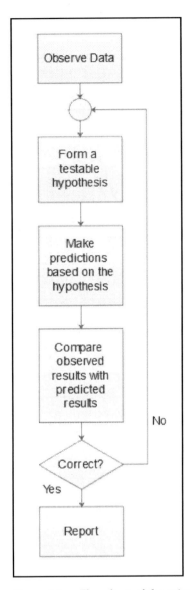

Figure 1.1 — Flowchart of the scientific method

A requirement of the scientific method is that the hypothesis is testable and is tested. A common error is to mistake the hypothesis to be an explanation of a phenomenon, exempt from performing tests—to believe that no test is needed.

An advantage of the scientific method is that it is unprejudiced. Faith, defined as belief that does not rest on logical proof or material evidence, is not required to determine whether to accept or reject the hypothesis. The results obtained using the scientific method are repeatable. It is not necessary to believe a published result; the reader can redo the experiment and replicate the result.

Importantly:

- The scientific method is rule-based and can be replicated. Given the model and the data, the results obtained are always the same without regard for who performs the tests or what his or her biases and subjective judgements might be.
- The model might consist of rules that are understandable, but that is not a requirement. Even if the rules are understandable, there is no requirement that they are in agreement with a previously defined body of cause-and-effect.

Software Engineering

Scientists study how nature works. Engineers create new things. Because their objectives are different, we might expect the processes used to be different. But the steps followed in the process of an engineering design are very similar to those of the scientific method.

- Define the problem.
- Specify requirements.
- Prototype alternative solutions.
- Test.
- Redesign as necessary.

Data Science

The term *data science* is in current favor to describe processes similar to the scientific method. One in particular, *CRISP-DM*, (Cross Industry Standard Process for Data Mining) describes steps of a data science lifecycle[4]:

- Business understanding.
- Data understanding.
- Data preparation.
- Modeling.
- Evaluation.
- Deployment.

The CRISP-DM process had been a standard supported by an industry consortium Special Interest Group, but that has dissolved. In 2015, IBM introduced a new methodology called *ASUM*, Analytics Solutions Unified Method for Data Mining, which refines and extends CRISP-DM. The IBM announcement explains that ASUM continues to sup-

---

4   Wikipedia, https://en.wikipedia.org/wiki/
    Cross_Industry_Standard_Process_for_Data_Mining

port the strong analytics of CRISP-DM while introducing additional tasks and activities in the deployment phase.

The diagram[5] in Figure 1.2 representing the CRISP-DM process is adequate for our purposes.

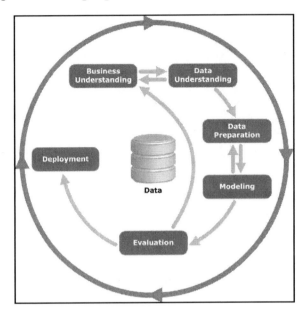

Figure 1.2 — The CRISP-DM process

The steps of data preparation, modeling, and evaluation are iterated until the results, based on evaluation of new and previously unused data, are satisfactory.

Trading System Development

Figure 1.3 shows the flowchart of the process of developing a trading system and its associated trading management system. The diagram clearly follows the scientific method, engineering process, and data science approach. It is the process discussed in this book.

- Observation and measurement of data. Analysis of historical data searching for patterns that precede profitable trades.
- Hypothesis statement and model specification. Define indicators, adjust parameters, propose rules that define trading signals, generate trades, analyze trades.
- Prediction and validation. Predict results for yet unseen data. Analyze accuracy of predictions.

---

5   Created by Kenneth Jensen, use per creative commons

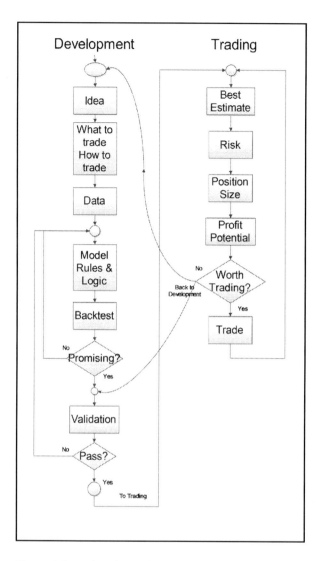

Figure 1.3 — Flowchart of trading system development
and trading management

Each Side of the Flowchart is a System

Trading system development has long been thought of as a relatively simple process of applying some chart pattern or indicator to a lengthy series of historical price data, often including a search for the best rules and parameter values, and often including calculation of the position size to be used for each trade.

As both the thinking about that process and the tools available for use with that process have evolved, we can develop better trading systems and better trading management systems by separating the single system into two distinct systems and applying the scientific method to each. Refer to Figure 1.3.

The development system is on the left side. It is what we think of as the trading system. Its input is one or more series of prices and its output is a series of buy and sell signals and the resulting trades. It handles design, testing, and validation of the trading model:
- Selecting the issue to trade.
- Selecting the auxiliary data.
- Processing of price and volume data.
- Calculating indicators.
- Establishing rules for trade entry and trade exit.
- Searching for profitable patterns.
- Generating trades.
- Computing metrics for measuring success.
- Creating many alternative models, searching for the best model.
- Testing to validate the pattern recognition.
- Establishing a baseline with which to compare future performance.

The trading management system is on the right side. It is in operation as the system is being traded live. Its input is a set of trades and its output is the position size for the next trade. It focuses on:
- Monitoring the health of the system being traded.
- Estimating risk.
- Determining maximum safe position size.
- Estimating profit potential.
- Determining whether to trade or take the system offline.
- Computing a metric with which to rank alternative systems to trade.

The two components share a common element—the set of trades that, during development, is the *best estimate* of future performance, and, during trading, is that best estimate set of trades augmented by trades actually taken.

System = Model + Data

As illustrated in Figure 1.4 a trading system is a combination of a model and some data.

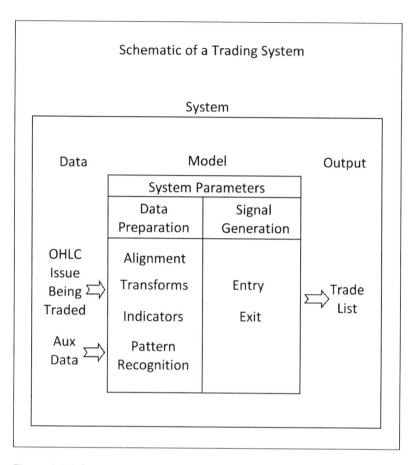

Figure 1.4 Schematic of a trading system

Models in General

The model accepts as input the data series that are being used. The data always includes a *primary series*—the issue being traded. It may also include auxiliary data, such as that used for inter-market analysis.

The model performs whatever data alignment and transformations are necessary. Parameters are chosen and indicators computed. The logic, rules, and parameters define patterns. When those patterns are found in the data, entry and exit signals are issued.

The purpose of the model is to recognize patterns that precede profitable trading opportunities.

The output from the model is a list of signals, with corresponding trades, for the time period being tested.

The model should not include any position sizing—that is handled in trading management. See the section Position Sizing below.

An Example Model

The logic:
- Use daily data bars.
- Evaluate at the close.
- Trade at the close.
- For every bar, compute the RSI indicator using a 3 bar lookback.
- For every bar, compute the value of the simple moving average of closing price using a 5 bar lookback.
- Issue a Buy signal when the RSI value falls from above 20 to below 20.
- Issue a Sell signal when the closing price moves from below its moving average to above.

This model uses two indicators:
- RSI—Relative Strength Indicator.
- Simple moving average.

It has three parameters:
- Lookback period for the RSI.
- Trigger level for Buy.
- Lookback period for the moving average.

It has two rules:
- Buy when the RSI falls through the trigger level.
- Sell when the closing price rises through the moving average.

The objective function is:
- CAR25

Note that the data series has not been specified. Data is not a component of the model.

This is one of many possible models. There are an infinite number of models that you could use.

Subjectivity and Objective Functions

Designing and developing trading systems, and trading, involves many decisions. Including:
- Which issue to trade.
- Which trading system to use.
- What logic, rules, and parameters are best.
- How long the system is stationary.
- How large a position to take.
- And many related decisions.

Discretionary traders acknowledge the subjectivity associated with those decisions and draw on their experience and judgement in making them.

Systematic traders use *objective functions* designed to identify important decision criteria, quantify them, and rank them. An objective function is alternatively called a loss function, cost function, utility function, fitness function, or optimization metric.

An objective function is a formula that includes terms for each of the criteria or variables important to the decision. Weights proportional to the importance of the criteria are given to each of the terms. The terms are combined together resulting in a single numeric quantity—an objective function score. The score is computed for each alternative being evaluated. The alternatives are sorted according to their score. Providing the objective function has been well designed, the order of the trader's subjective preference is the same as the order of objective function score.

Objective functions are important in both phases of trading:
• In development—to rank alternative systems.
• In trading management—to decide the size of the next position.

In the past, choices of objective function were limited to those provided by the platform. The early built-in metrics were limited and rigid, making it difficult for developers to match the objective function to their own preferences. Some rewarded the wrong characteristics giving high scores to systems that do not perform well out-of-sample, and making validation of the systems difficult.

The objective function must represent the subjectivity of the developer's definition of best. But it is important in other ways as well. Choice of the metric influences:
• The ranking of alternative systems.
• Selection of which one is best.
• Accuracy of estimates of risk and profit.
• Stability of the system as it is traded.

Modern platforms give developers much better tools. If you are able to create your own custom objective function, include terms that measure basic system performance, such as:
• Trading frequency.
• Accuracy.
• Holding period.
• Gain per trade.
• Amount lost on losing trades.

Objective function scores using these components will have the same value no matter the order of occurrence of the trades.

Avoid terms that are sequence dependent—that will change if the trades occur in a different order—such as maximum drawdown, or any of the ratios that include drawdown.

I have developed an objective function that is nearly universal. I call it CAR25. It is described in the section CAR25 below. If calculation of CAR25 is within the capabilities of the platform you are using, I recommend you use it. Or at least try it. If not, use the best of the metrics available in your platform.

The Data

Primary data

The primary data series is a time-ordered sequence of quotations. Each quotation represents the price of the issue being traded. The prices can be:

- Individual transaction prices—ticks.
- Individual quotations—bid and ask.
- A set of values that provide the range of prices for some period of time—a bar.

The data format assumed throughout this book is bars. Each bar represents a fixed length of time and is a set of numbers that specify the prices associated with that bar. When the issue is a stock, ETF, or commodity, the prices typically include the first, highest, lowest, and last for that period, referred to as open, high, low, and close. Note that, in general, we cannot assume that the first price occurred at the time the bar opened, nor that the last price occurred at the time the bar closed. We never know, nor should we assume, anything about the order of prices within the bar. Specifically, without examining bars of shorter time duration within a longer bar, we cannot determine whether the high came before the low or after it.

In some cases, such as with stocks and ETFs, the volume of shares is also included and reported.

The most common bar length is one trading day, in which case the data is described as being *daily bars* or *end-of-day* data. Bars can be as short as one second, or a few seconds, one minute, or some number of minutes. Any of these is described as *intra-day* data or intra-day bars.

When buy and sell signals are issued and trades created, the transaction prices come from this primary data series.

Auxiliary data

In addition to the prices of the issue being traded, the model might use auxiliary data. That could be the price of other tradable issues—for example, including the price of bonds in a model that trades stocks. Or it could be a non-price series—for example, the number of advancing or declining issues from a broader set, such as a market sector.

Data munging[6]

Before being analyzed, all data series must be aligned by the date and time associated with each bar, and any missing data filled in. The obvious choice to provide the master list of dates and times is the primary data series.

At a minimum:
- All series and fields referenced by the model must be present in the data.
- All data series used must be aligned to the same periodicity and the same time zone.
- All missing data must be filled in—copied forward as necessary.

Sound business practice suggests that the data also:
- Be current.
- Be reported by an independent clearing agency.
- Be the public record of trades freely made between willing parties.
- Be reported to the public no later than to any other private parties.
- Have the same level of revision history in both development and trading.

These requirements imply consequences for several categories of data.

Fundamental Data

Data representing company fundamentals and economic series is of little use in the systems discussed here. See Appendix A for more details.

Simulated Data

Artificial data, random data, simulated data, or data generated from a standard distribution is of very limited value. Real trades result only when a pattern is detected in the real data being processed. In order to be useful in training, the training data must contain instances of the pattern. If we knew the pattern accurately enough to be able to create useful training data, we would already have the information we needed to define the rules, and we would not need any development.

Over-the-counter Data

These include:

---

6   Data munging or data wrangling is loosely the process of manually converting or mapping data from one "raw" form into another format that allows for more convenient consumption of the data with the help of semi-automated tools.

- Transactions between private parties.
- Bids and offers not open to the public.
- Transactions not recorded by an independent clearing agency.
- Transactions reported to a limited audience before being reported publicly.
- Records changed after initial reporting.

All of these characteristics are faults and skew the advantage toward a potentially biased counterparty.

Synchronization

The model specifies the logic, rules, and parameters. The rules, for example, might be to enter and exit as two moving averages cross. The parameters include the lengths of the two moving averages.

The data is the price history of the issue being traded, perhaps augmented by other data series.

A trading system is profitable as long as the logic identifies patterns in the data that precede profitable trading opportunities. That is, as long as the logic and data remain synchronized.

The logic of a typical trading system is relatively fixed. It is designed to detect a particular set of patterns. The data change, following changes in areas that affect the issue—economics, politics, weather, etc.

As the data changes, the patterns in the data move in and out of synchronization with the logic. When synchronized, the system is healthy, it is profitable, gains are steady, drawdowns are low; when unsynchronized, the system is broken, it is unprofitable, gains are sporadic, drawdowns are high. The profit potential and drawdown risk of a system are determined by the accuracy with which the system identifies the patterns.

During periods of close synchronization, the system is healthy and large positions may safely be taken. As synchronization weakens, position size must be reduced.

Stationarity

Stationarity is a feature of data that refers to how a particular metric of the data remains relatively constant or changes as different subsets of the data are analyzed.

A process, or set of data, is described as *strictly* or *strongly* stationary when the distribution and its parameters—such as mean, variance, skew, and kurtosis—do not change over time, including showing no trends. Stationarity is a required assumption for some analysis techniques.

The techniques discussed in this book extend the concept of stationarity to whatever metric is being analyzed. In particular, we will pay careful attention to the relationship between critical patterns and the trades that follow. We want that relationship to remain stationary.

Traditional statistical analysis, including much of both probability and machine learning, assumes the data being analyzed is strongly stationary. (More about machine learning in Chapter 3.) The theorems upon which the techniques are based, in particular those that give limits to accuracy and / or error, often require strong stationarity. That assumption is reasonable for applications such as political polling, medical diagnosis, and character recognition.

But time series data is seldom stationary, and financial time series data is particularly non-stationary. Be cautious when applying any technique that assumes the data is stationary to financial time series—there will probably be an undesirable bias.

Watch the video of a presentation I made about stationarity and posted to YouTube[7].

The Signal and the Noise

The data is a series of prices of transactions in order by date and time. If our trading system is to be profitable, the model we use to analyze that data must recognize patterns in that data that precede profitable trades. Those patterns are the signal.

In our lives, we are surrounded by data from which we must isolate and identify meaningful signals. We pick out words in conversations from the background of sounds, traffic signs from the clutter of images, individual faces from a crowd. In all of these, we are extracting the signal from the data, ignoring the noise. Our understanding of the signal and our proper response to it depends on the *real* or *true* signal being clear and strong, with little interference or confusion from *imaginary* or *false* signals caused by randomness and artifacts in the background noise.

Traffic signs are designed to stand out clearly and be easily recognized. The picture on a television set is clear and crisp. In these examples, we say that the signal to noise ratio is high. There are few false signals in the background. To aid traffic safety, distracting signs are removed. To ensure viewer satisfaction, static is filtered out.

Financial data is different. While the success of our trading systems depend on the existence of real signals, those signals are not clear. The signal to noise ratio is low. There are many false signals. There is a great deal of ambiguity and contradictory data. There is no agency

---

7   *The Importance of Being Stationary,*
    https://www.youtube.com/watch?v=iBhrZKErJ6A&feature=y
    outu.be

charged with cleaning up the background or enhancing the signal. Being able to identify profitable signals has a high monetary value and sharing those signals dilutes their value, so no rational agent has an incentive to improve the ease with which the signal can be identified.

The elusiveness of profitable signals means that developers of trading systems must do everything they can to ensure their model is recognizing persistent, profitable patterns. They must follow the scientific method. They must validate rigorously.

For a book-length discussion of this topic, read Nate Silver, *The Signal and the Noise*[8].

Every Model-Data Combination is a System

For a given model, when the primary data series is SPY, that defines one trading system. When the primary data series is IBM, that defines a second trading system.

When any of the indicators, parameters, or rules change, or the data series changes, the result is a new system. Each of these systems is an alternative that might be tradable. One of them is the best of the alternatives. The development process seeks to identify the best one—the one that gives the highest return relative to risk.

You will be defining, testing, and evaluating many thousands of alternative systems. The diagram in Figure 1.5 shows five models and four data series, resulting in 20 separate systems.

	ABC L/F	ABC S/F	DEF L/F	ABC-DEF Pair
Mean Reversion RSI(2)				
Mean Reversion RSI(3)				
Break Out 20 Day High				
MA Cross -- 5 & 20				
MA Cross -- 50 and 200				

Figure 1.5 20 alternative trading systems

Each cell is a system—a combination of a model and some data. Mean Reversion RSI(2) is a model that enters when the 2 period RSI meets some condition. Break Out 20 Day High is a model that enters when

8   https://www.amazon.com/Signal-
    Noise-Many-Predictions-Fail--but/
    dp/0143125087/

the issue closes at a new high for the most recent 20 days. Changing anything in a model creates a new model and adds a row.

ABC L/F is the common stock with ticker symbol ABC, traded long and flat. ABC S/F is the common stock with the symbol ABC, traded short and flat. Using a different data series adds a column.

Changing anything in a model—an indicator, a parameter, a trigger level—creates a new and separate model. Applying a model to a different data series creates a different system.

Each is an alternative that must be evaluated as to its profit potential and validated as to its likelihood to be profitable in the future. An immediate question is "which is best?" Followed by "what metric should I use?"

In order to compare alternatives, there must be a way to normalize them—something that establishes the "everything else being equal" part of any comparative ranking. We will normalize relative to risk.

Data Series are Not Interchangeable

It is the combination of a model and some data that comprise a trading system.

Just as we cannot expect different models to be equally effective for a given data series, we cannot expect a given model to be equally effective applied to different data series. If one model does work for a wide range of data, that is a plus. But it is not a requirement.

Development

Developing trading systems is in many ways similar to developing systems that predict the likelihood of a default on a loan given data about the borrower. Or the identification of the species of a flower given data about its petals and leaves.

All follow the same method—the scientific method:
- Analyze data searching for patterns.
- Write rules that define what has been learned.
- Test on new data to validate that the system works.
- Put the system into practice.

Developing trading systems is more complicated for several reasons.

For systems such as flower identification or credit scoring:
- Input data is characteristics of the physical item or personal behavior.
- Data is not time series. The order of the data points is not important.

- Data is stationary. The distribution of the data is stable over reasonably long periods of time. Any given subset of the data is similar to any other subset.
- Data is self-contained. Data points are independent of each other.
- Data and model are well behaved.
- Data has a high signal to noise ratio.
- Data is unaffected by use of the model describing it.
- Output is the category or value related to the data.

For a trading system:
- Input data is price and volume of the issue being traded.
- Data is time series. The order of the data points is important and must be accommodated.
- Data is not stationary. The distribution changes over time. The model must recognize changes and adapt by itself, or be recalibrated by the developer, as the distribution changes.
- Data is not independent. Trading system models often compare current values with previous values.
- Data is often volatile and ambiguous.
- Data has a low signal to noise ratio.
- The data changes as the system is used and because it is used. Profitable use causes the issue to be more efficient, the model to be more difficult to fit, and future trades less profitable.
- Output is signals and trades.

For a trading management system:
- Input data is trades.
- Data is time series.
- Data is not directly related to the trading system that produces the trades.
- Data is not stationary.
- Produces position size, metric of system health, and metric of risk-normalized profitability as its output.

The Process

This is a classical example of fitting a model to a set of data, intending to use the model for prediction.

In order to have a system that generates signals that we have confidence in, that is profitable, and that has acceptable risk, we need several things:
- Data series that have enough variation so that buying and selling produces profit in excess of risk-free alternative uses of the money.
- Those same data series must not have so much volatility that the resulting system has risk of drawdown that exceeds the trader's personal risk tolerance.

- Existence of patterns in the data that precede profitable trading opportunities.
- Existence of a set of rules and parameters, call it a model, that recognizes the patterns and issues trading signals.
- Our ability to discover the model and verify that it works for historical data, creating a trading system.
- Our ability to monitor the performance of the trades generated by the system over time to verify that the system has learned to recognize the patterns and that the patterns continue.
- Our ability to compute the correct position size for each trade so that we maximize account growth while holding drawdown within personal limits of risk tolerance.
- Our ability to recognize system breakdown and take the system offline before excessive loss of trading capital.

Refer to the development side of the flowchart in Figure 1.3. There is a cycle, often extensive, where the two steps of refine the model and test its performance are repeated until the model fits the data and the trades are profitable. The data used for this portion is called the *in-sample* data. Because the signal to noise ratio of true signals is so low, the in-sample results are often based more on fitting the model to the specific data, including noise, rather than fitting to true, persistent signals that will be profitable in the future. In-sample results have very little value in evaluating a system. They always underestimate risk and overestimate profit.

It is only through validation—testing using data that has not previous been used, called the *out-of-sample* data—that we can estimate whether the system learned and is potentially profitable or was only *curve-fit* to the data.

Developers should note that making multiple passes through the entire develop and validate procedure, adjusting the model based on out-of-sample results, converts the previously out-of-sample data into in-sample data, requiring a new set of validation data.

Distributions

Stationarity is a condition of a distribution. The distribution we care about is of signals and trades.

In fact, the entire purpose of trading system development is to learn as much as possible about the distribution of signals and trades.

The best we can hope for is that the distribution of trades in the future will resemble the distribution of trades in the past. That they will have the same frequency, accuracy, mean, variance, and other important statistics. That the cumulative distribution functions are the same. We cannot expect the same trades in the same order. Since drawdown is a sequence-dependent metric, we cannot expect the same drawdown.

Because of the way we test and evaluate trading systems, the in-sample test result that catches our eye is always better than average. Be prepared for validation and live trading results to be less optimistic.

The information content that describes a trading system over a given period of time can be described in many ways. The following list is in decreasing order of information.
- Reality. Trades, in sequence, that actually result from applying the system.
- List of trades, in time sequence.
- Set of trades.
- Distribution of trades.
- Four moments describing the distribution.
- Mean and standard deviation.
- Mean.
- Direction.

Probability and statistics distinguish between population and sample. The population is all items of the type being analyzed. The sample is a subset of the population that has been observed. The purpose of developing trading systems is to learn as much as possible about the population of trades that will occur in the future and make estimates of future performance. The results of testing trading systems form the sample that is used to make those estimates.

Reality

Reality cannot be known in advance. Estimating reality, the population, is the purpose of system validation. Reality is the logic of the system processing the future data series.

List of trades, in time sequence

The list of trades, in time sequence, that results from processing a data series that is similar to the future data, is the best estimate we can obtain of reality. There is one of these sequences for each unique series of test data and each set of logic and parameter values. Using these results to estimate future profitability and risk depends on the degree of similarity between the test data and the future data.

Set of trades

The set of trades, ignoring time sequence, relaxes the assumption of the trades occurring in a particular sequence. It provides a set of trade data with, hopefully, the same characteristics as the future data, such as amount won or lost per trade, holding period, intra-trade drawdown, and frequency of trading. Selecting trades from this set in random order gives an opportunity to evaluate the effects of similar conditions, but in different time sequence.

Distribution of trades

A distribution can be formed using any of the metrics of the individual trades. The distribution is a further simplification since there are fewer (or at most the same number of) categories for the distribution than for the data used to form it. For example, a distribution of percentage gain per trade is formed by sorting the individual trades according to gain per trade, establishing ranges and bins, assigning each trade to a bin, and counting the number of trades in each bin. A plot of the count per bin versus gain per bin gives a plot of the probability mass function (called the probability density function, pdf, when the data is continuous).

A measurement without an estimate of its accuracy is of limited value. Distributions are excellent tools for estimating accuracy and providing visual displays.

Four moments

Distributions can be described by their moments. The four moments most commonly used are named mean, variance, skewness, and kurtosis. Depending on the distribution, some or all of the moments may be undefined.
- Mean. The first moment. The arithmetic average of the data points.
- Variance. Second moment. A measure of the deviation of data points from the mean. Standard deviation is the positive square root of variance.
- Skewness. Third moment. A measure of the lopsidedness of the distribution.
- Kurtosis. Fourth moment. A measure of the peakedness and tail weight of the distribution.

Mean and standard deviation

Mean and standard deviation are commonly computed and used to describe trade results. They can be used in the definition of metrics such Bollinger bands, z-score, Sharpe ratio, mean-variance portfolio, etc.

Mean

The mean gives the average of the values. Mean can be computed in several ways, such as arithmetic mean and geometric mean. Median is an alternative measure of central tendency of a sample that is often useful.

Direction

Direction of a trade describes whether it was a winning trade or a losing trade. Direction is meant to represent any way of describing the trades in a binary fashion. Other ways might be whether the result was large or small in absolute value, or whether the maximum favorable excursion met some criterion, etc.

Stay High on the List

With each step down this list, a larger number of data points are consolidated into a smaller number of categories, and information is irretrievably lost. Knowing only the information available at one level makes it impossible to know anything definite about the population that could be determined at a higher level. Working with only the mean tells us nothing about variability. Working with only mean and standard deviation tells us nothing about the heaviness of the tails. Using the four values of the first four moments enables us to calculate some information about the shape of the population, but nothing about the lumpiness or gaps that may exist.

There are several books listed in the bibliography that have excellent discussion of the importance of distributions and the dangers of using only single values. Good books to begin with those of Sam Savage[9] and Patrick Leach.[10]

Choosing the trades that comprise the sample we use to approximate the population is critically important.

For each alternative, decide what set of trades is the best estimate of future performance. If available, use actual trades. Next best is paper trades from a system that has passed validation. Or the set of trades from the walk forward runs of a validation process. The process works for any set of trades, even some that are entirely hypothetical or that come from in-sample testing. The reliability of the result depends on the quality of the estimated trades.

Assume Nothing About the Distribution

Numerous studies have documented that financial data does not reliably follow any of the standard statistical distributions. In general, we do not know—or even need to know—the distribution of the data. It is important to accept and use the data as it is without making additional assumptions as to being normal, log-normal, or any other distribution.

Position sizing

Position sizing—determining the number of shares or contracts for the next trade—is vitally important. Risk of account-destroying draw-

9   Savage, Sam, *The Flaw of Averages: Why We Underestimate Risk in the Face of Uncertainty*, Wiley, 2009.

10 Leach, Patrick, *Why Can't You Just Give Me the Number?*, Probabilistic Publishing, 2006.

down and opportunity for account-growing profit are closely linked, with position size the critical and coordinating variable.

Position size calculations are based on the distribution of trades.

Position size should not be a component of the trading model itself. Including it there causes two problems:
1. During development of the trading system. Using position size other than a fixed number of contracts or dollars introduces a bias that favors specific models that benefit from specific order of trades that happen to occur in the historical data used for development, but are unlikely to be repeated in the future.
2. During trading of the system.
   A. Assuming that position size is constant implies that the distribution of trades is stationary—an assumption that is seldom correct.
   B. The trading system has a large number of rules and parameters that can be varied in the search for the best system. The management system has only one—position size. Including position size in the trading system removes it from the management system, leaving no variable that can be used for objective trading management.

Part of the problem of where to put position size calculation was, in the past, due to limitations of the trading system development platforms.

Trading system development platforms are very good at processing price data, producing a trade sequence, and computing single-valued metrics. But relatively poor at the complex mathematics and Monte Carlo simulations required to estimate and analyze distributions related to the trades. Until recently, there was little choice. Either include position size in the trading system or deal with it using a separate process and a separate analysis program—perhaps a spreadsheet.

The technological barriers to more accurately modeling trading systems and trading management are being removed. Recent advances in software have provided new opportunities. Trading system development platforms, such as AmiBroker, now have built-in Monte Carlo functions. General purpose languages, such as Python, have been augmented with libraries such as Pandas to ease the handling of time series data, libraries such as NumPy and SciPy to ease complex mathematics and Monte Carlo simulations, and libraries such as Scikit-learn to assist in pattern recognition and classification. Python can be used as the platform for both development and management.

Risk Tolerance

Every trader has a personal tolerance for risk. Every data series has some inherent risk, independent of the model. Every trading system has some risk.

One of the features of risk analysis is a metric that enables alternative uses of funds to be compared on an equal basis. The process is *risk-normalization*. The metric is *safe-f*. Chapter 2 describes the process, the metric, its computation, and its use. Here is a brief introduction to the process.

Begin with a statement of personal risk tolerance. An example is:

> I am trading a $100,000 account and forecasting two years into the future. I want to hold the risk of a drawdown in my trading account of 20% or greater to a chance of 5% or less.

Every trading system goes through periods of good performance and poor performance as the model and the data move in and out of synchronization—signals are accurate and signals are inaccurate. The inaccurate signals and periods of poor performance result in a drawdown of the trading account.

We each have some level of risk we are willing to tolerate before we admit that the system is not working and must be taken offline in order to preserve trading capital. It is the maximum drawdown stated in our risk tolerance statement.

The drawdown from the trading system is the result of one set of trades in a specific sequence. That one trade sequence and equity curve are one of many possible sequences and equity curves drawn from that same sample of signals and trades. Together, they form a distribution of equity curves, each with its own drawdown, associated with that set of trades and the permutations of the order of the trades. We can compute the depth of drawdowns of that distribution, and learn the relationship between drawdown and position size. Position size, safe-f, is adjusted so that the drawdowns remain within our tolerance.

Interestingly, each tradable issue has inherent risk (and inherent profit potential) based on its volatility. The risk-normalization procedure can assess the probable profitability of trading that issue even before a model is applied. Chapter 2 has details.

Dynamic Position Sizing

If a trading system was stationary, we could rely on recovery from drawdowns based on the law of large numbers. We would just keep trading, anticipating the losing period would be followed by a winning period, with an eventual return to the average expectation.

But systems are not stationary. When the system was developed and validated, the model was tuned to recognize the then-current signals in the data. If—more likely when—the data changes, the model is unable to adjust sufficiently and performance deteriorates. We have no way of distinguishing between a small drawdown that is normal given the distribution of trading observed during development and the beginning of an account-destroying drawdown because of a major change in the system. The proper and prudent management action is to reduce position size in response to periods of poor performance and increase position size in response to good performance.

The procedure that I call *dynamic position sizing* uses recent trades to estimate the drawdown projected for a future period.
- System performance is monitored trade by trade.
- A Monte Carlo procedure generates many possible and equally likely future trade sequences.
- The distribution of maximum drawdown is formed.
- Position size is adjusted so that drawdown equals the trader's personal risk tolerance. The position size that makes that adjustment is called *safe-f*—the maximum safe position size for the next trade.

Safe-f gives you a clear indication of system health, including when the system should be taken offline.

My *Quantitative Technical Analysis* book has details and runable code.

CAR25—Universal Objective Function

The position size for the next trade is safe-f. Trading at the given safe-f, we can estimate the account balance for the future period. Account balance is converted to a metric that represents the compound annual rate of return for the system. I call that metric *CAR25*.

CAR25 is the credible value of expected equity growth associated with the risk-normalized forecast of a trading system. It is the most universal objective function for trading system development and trading management I have found.

Given this procedure, all alternatives can have their risk-normalized CAR25 computed. Since risk of drawdown is the limiting factor, and risk of drawdown is the same for all the alternatives, the alternative to trade is the one with the highest CAR25.

If CAR25 is below the return of other alternative uses of the funds in the trading account, take the system offline and use the funds in some other way.

Estimating Future Performance

The development platform's report shows a list of trades, a single equity curve, with a single maximum drawdown. The equity curve and drawdown are computed using the trades in the test period in the sequence they occurred in the test period.

These results will be repeated when the system is traded only if future prices are exactly the same as the historical series used during development. In order to estimate profit potential and risk it is important to consider the distribution of potential results.

Modeling future performance, including evaluating system health, estimating risk, and estimating profit potential, is based on:

- Using the set of trade results that best represents the trades that are likely to occur in the future.
- Using Monte Carlo simulation techniques to create many equally likely trade sequences.
- Analyzing the distributions of drawdown and profit resulting from the trade sequences.
- Comparing both the magnitude and probability of both the drawdown and profit potential with the trader's personal tolerance for risk and desire for profit to determine system health and position size.

The model and the data must remain synchronized for the period of development and into trading. Recall the premise of technical analysis —"the future resembles the present."

Trader Psychology

We often hear of the importance of psychology in successful trading. The need for the trader to understand himself, to trust the system, to take all signals, to enter the market when the buy signal appears, to set stops at a comfortable level, to exit the trade when the money management stop is hit, to exit the trade at a profit when the profit target is hit, to keep trading through drawdowns. And if the trader considers second-guessing the system, he should consult a trading coach to help him realign his beliefs and accept the system.

In my opinion, that is exactly backwards. We all have personal beliefs about the way the markets work, comfort levels with risk, and preferences related to trading. We know what trading frequency fits in with our other activities. We know what level of drawdown causes us to lose sleep. We can incorporate our own preferences into the objective function we design for our own use when developing and trading our own systems. We can monitor system performance trade by trade and adjust position size accordingly.

A system that scores high marks using our own custom objective function is already one we can expect to be comfortable using. A well designed custom objective function together with dynamic position sizing go a long way toward avoiding the cognitive dissonance that requires professional consultation to cure.

Confidence

In the end, you must have confidence. If not confidence, then faith— belief without supporting evidence.

The forums that discuss trading systems and their development often ask about the value of walk forward testing. The question is usually accompanied by comments about how hard it is to get good results from the out-of-sample tests from the walk forward[11] runs, whereas it is relatively easy to get good results from optimization and backtesting.

My first reaction is the obvious one—it is hard to get good out-of-sample results because the markets are nearly efficient and it is hard to write a set of rules that identify a weak signal in a noisy background.

But the first question leads to a deeper consideration about trading systems and trading. Having confidence in a system.

It is my view that the universe of trading system application divides into two—having confidence and having faith.

If you want quantifiable confidence—the kind that tells you whether to hit soft 17 at blackjack, or to hit the blot in your inner table in backgammon, or to buy a recent low, or to buy a new high breakout—my techniques are designed to provide quantifiable confidence in both development and trading.

The problem is harder than it looks at first blush. The characteristics of a trading system determine to a large extent whether it is even possible to have confidence. In order to be useful, there must be enough data points—closed trades or daily account equity values—to compute useful statistical metrics. Examples of useful statements about confidence are:

• To put a low p-value on a set of system results, such as: "we can reject the hypothesis that the expectancy is less than 0.0 with a p-value of 0.05."
• To put limits on estimates, such as: "with 95% confidence, the worst maximum drawdown for the next year for an account with an initial balance of $100,000 trading at a fraction of 0.80 is 20%."

Statistical metrics such as these can be computed for any data set—real or hypothetical. If future trades will be made based on these statistics, the data set used to compute the test statistics must be as unbiased as possible.

Using the walk forward technique with trading systems that trade frequently and have short holding periods gives the trading system developer a reasonable chance of producing a set of trades that is both large enough and unbiased enough. Even at that, it is all too easy to introduce bias—bias that will cause reward to be overestimated and risk underestimated—into even the walk forward out-of-sample results.

Compare with backtesting with little or no out-of-sample testing, (which is the all-too-common method in both the popular trading jour-

---

11 Explained in Chapter 3 — Development

nals and many professional publications), or with systems that have such long holding periods or infrequent trading that an unbiased data set cannot, for practical purposes, be produced.

When in doubt, test it! Do not accept traditional wisdom blindly. Is the 200 day moving average a good trend indicator? Do Gann indicators have predictive value? Is long-term holding the best system to grow a trading account with low drawdown? Those rules may be good ones, and they may lead to trading systems that are appropriate for your use. Or they may not.

Beware of following the advice of the White Queen: "Why, sometimes I've believed as many as six impossible things before breakfast."[12]

Test everything yourself. Your logic, your data, your execution, your estimation of system health. If those tests give you confidence, act accordingly. Remember to reserve some data for one-time out-of-sample testing. In-sample results always underestimate risk and overestimate profit. If you do not perform out-of-sample testing yourself, the market will do it for you, using real money.

If you must act on faith, ask yourself how the casino can build such a fine facility. Stand next to the roulette wheel and listen to the young man tell his partner: "There have been six reds in a row. Black is due." (He might have said the same thing after 4 reds, then after 5 reds, as well.)

Skill Set

Trading system development can be described by any of several names:
* Artificial intelligence.
* Data analysis.
* Data mining.
* Data science.
* Machine learning.
* Modeling and simulation.
* Pattern recognition.
* Predictive analytics.
* Statistical inference.

Whatever name you give it, successful application requires expertise in three areas:
* Domain knowledge.
* Computer programming.
* Mathematics and statistics.

Domain knowledge relates to the subject being modeled. Understanding financial instruments in general, and specifics related to whichever

---

12 Carroll, Lewis, *Through the Looking-Glass*, 1871.

stocks, mutual funds, exchange traded funds, futures, or currencies will be traded.

Computer programming to implement the tasks of data access, data cleaning, transformations, preparations for passing the data to the modeling software, and running the modeling software.

Mathematics in support of data preparation prior to modeling and statistics in support of interpretation of results.

Monte Carlo—Briefly

The Monte Carlo simulation technique repeatedly builds and analyzes a sequence of trades. Each sequence represents a fixed time horizon, say two years. The number of trades in that sequence is the number of trades that can be expected to occur in two years. Each trade is selected from either a trade list or a distribution that represents a trade list. When enough trades to cover two years have been selected, the equity curve, win-to-loss ratio, maximum drawdown, and other metrics of interest can be calculated–just as if this sequence was a two-year trade history.

After generating and analyzing many, usually thousands, of two-year sequences, form and analyze the distributions of the results. Two of the most important metrics of results are maximum closed trade drawdown, which leads to safe-f and account growth which leads to CAR25. Others that might be of interest include win-to-loss ratio, maximum intra-trade drawdown, etc.

The important points are:
*   Use the best data available. Out-of-sample data that best represents the anticipated future data that will be traded.
*   Use the highest representation of the data possible. That is, either a list of trades or a detailed distribution of trades.
*   Using simulation techniques, generate many possible trade sequences.
*   Analyze the distributions of the results of the simulation.
*   Calculate and use metrics based on the distributions to judge the usefulness of the system.

Why This is So Hard

Developing profitable trading systems is a difficult problem for many reasons.

Low Signal to Noise Ratio

The data is very noisy. The markets are nearly efficient. Thinking of the patterns we are searching for as the signal, the signal is weak and is hidden among a lot of noise.

Nonstationary

The data is not stationary. Nothing stays the same for long. The characteristics of the data change over time. A solution found for one period of time may no longer apply in a later time period. Determining the appropriate lengths of time to use for the in-sample and out-of-sample periods is difficult.

Time Series is Different

Time series data, and particularly financial time series data, is different than the data typically fed to models. The vast majority of modeling, simulation, statistics, and machine learning books and articles assume the data is stationary.

When it is, models that learn and predict accurately are relatively easy to build. The theory provides guidelines, and in some cases rigorous estimates, of out-of-sample performance.

When it is not, techniques that rely on stationarity still give results. But the theoretical justification fails to hold. Results overestimate profit and underestimate risk. Real-time trading results are much poorer than anticipated.

Feedback

The purpose of a trading system is to recognize an inefficiency in price, then make trades that capture that inefficiency. An example is the process described as "arbitraging an inefficiency out of the system." In the process, price becomes more efficient and more difficult to detect in the future.

Trend Following

Every trade is a trend following trade. No matter how the entry is made, the price must change in the direction predicted in order for the system to be profitable. The trend must complete its expected or predicted run before there is a drawdown or early exit from the trade. As more traders recognize that particular trending pattern, the trend becomes shorter in both time and price change.

Limited Profit Potential

The markets are very nearly efficient. Every successful trade removes some inefficiency and makes future profitability less likely. Given a desirable trend, the first positions taken get the best price. Later fills are at worse prices. The latest trades do not obtain enough profit to cover commission and slippage.

Different Systems, Same Trades

Trades can be categorized according to the amount of change from entry to exit, or the amount of time they are held. Over a period of time, there are only a few profitable trades for any given trade profile. Everyone developing systems that will hold trades for one to five days or one to two percent will locate the same profitable trades no matter what pattern or entry technique they are using.

Very Large Search Space

There are many potential solutions. Patterns can be described in terms of indicators, seasonality, candles, etc. Finding a pattern that works is a search among a large number of possibilities. It is very easy to overfit the model to the data.

The in-sample results are always good. With so many variables available to fit so few data points, it is easy to obtain good in-sample results.

Out-of-sample Results Matter

Out-of-sample results are the important ones. They may not be good for two reasons.
- One. The system was never good. The rules fit the in-sample noise rather than meaningful and predictive patterns.
- Two. The system is no longer good. The characteristics of the data have changed since the patterns were identified.

Financial Rewards

Rewards for success are high.

Barriers to entry are low.

Trading is competitive. Trading is nearly zero sum. My profit is some other trader's loss. Knowledge shared by one trader reduces his future profit.

Competition

There are no handicaps. Novice and journeyman golfers, bowlers, tennis players, chess players, bicycle racers, and go players can all enter tournaments knowing that they will either be competing with people whose skill level is roughly the same as their own, or they will be given a handicap that compensates for their lack of skill and experience. Not so for traders. When any of us takes a long position in a stock, ETF, or futures contract, the person taking the opposite position is very likely to be trading for a major financial institution. They are well educated, well equipped, well funded, well supported, and are using the best methods and systems.

Figure 1.6 After I win a few races, I am going to buy a really good bicycle and enter the Tour de France.

Summary

The systems we develop will be quantitative. At every point in their development and use, there will be metrics to help make decisions.

Many trading decisions are subjective. We will use objective functions to quantify subjective preferences.

The system's characteristics are determined in part by the desires of the trader and in part by what is achievable within the specified risk tolerance. They are also determined by, and to some extent restricted by, the practicalities and realities of combining sound practices of mathematical modeling, simulation, and statistical analysis with uniqueness of financial time series and the business of trading.

George Box famously wrote: "Essentially all models are wrong, but some are useful."[13] The more complete quotation adds some qualifications, including: "all models are approximations." Understanding that trading systems are not perfect, my hope is to help you develop systems that are useful.

Data has been, is, and forever will be, at the heart of science. The scientific method, engineering process, and practice of data science are all based on extracting knowledge from data.

Several hedge funds use quantitative methods to manage large amounts of money and achieve respectable profits. We can take that as evidence that what we hope to do is possible. Examples include:
- Renaissance Technologies, James Simons.
- D. E. Shaw Group, David Shaw.

---

13 Box, G. E. P., and Draper, N. R., *Empirical Model Building and Response Surfaces*, John Wiley & Sons, New York, NY, 1987.

Chapter 2 — Risk

The primary reason traders stop trading a system is that they experience a drawdown larger than they anticipated, larger than they can afford, larger than their risk tolerance.

To manage risk, we must first measure it.

We begin with some definitions. Then use the list of trades produced by specific test runs to illustrate how:
- Risk is measured and quantified.
- The distribution of risk is plotted.
- The highest safe position size, safe-f, is calculated.
- Results are normalized relative to risk.
- Risk-normalized profit potential, CAR25, is estimated.
- CAR25 is used to compare alternatives.

Definitions

We begin with a discussion of drawdown as a measure of risk, analysis of the visibility of intra-trade prices, and willingness to hold a position through a drawdown.

Drawdown Defined

Drawdown is defined as the drop in account equity, measured as a percentage relative to the highest equity achieved prior to the drawdown. Figure 2.1 shows two major drawdowns—one of 10% and one of 20%.

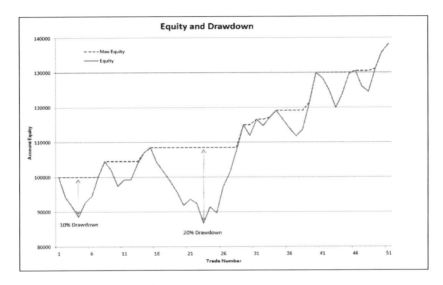

Figure 2.1 Account drawdown

As Figure 2.2 illustrates, loss of equity into a drawdown is not symmetric with the gain required to recover from it. The gain needed to recover from a drawdown is greater than the loss that caused the drawdown.

Figure 2.2 also illustrates another view of drawdown—the time required to recover. Assuming a system has an expected annual growth of 15%, recovery from a 20% drawdown will take about 20 months.

It is one thing to look at a chart showing an historical record. Perhaps of a trading system, perhaps of a broad market index, perhaps of a country's economy. The chart shows several deep drawdowns, each followed by recovery. The person imagines the final outcome and believes any current drawdown in a system, market, or economy will be followed by an equally full and pleasant recovery. It is both easy and patriotic to have faith in a recovery, but painful to personally experience the discomfort throughout the entire period. Every forecast should include consideration of how it might be different this time—or not different, as the case may be.

Drawdown percent	Recovery percent	Recovery months at 15%
1%	1.01%	0.8
2%	2.04%	1.6
3%	3.09%	2.5
4%	4.17%	3.3
5%	5.26%	4.2
6%	6.38%	5.1
7%	7.53%	6.0
8%	8.70%	7.0
9%	9.89%	7.9
10%	11.11%	8.9
15%	17.65%	14.1
20%	25.00%	20.0
30%	42.86%	34.3
40%	66.67%	53.3
50%	100.00%	80.0
60%	150.00%	120.0

Figure 2.2 Drawdown and recovery

Frequency of Action

A system's equity is either at a new high, or it is in a drawdown. Most systems are in drawdowns most of the time—70 to 90% of the time is not unusual.

Continuing to trade a system that is in a drawdown requires that you have confidence that:
1. The drawdown is within your risk tolerance.
2. Compared with the trading history and expected performance, the current drawdown is not unusually deep or long.
3. The system will recover to make a new equity high in a reasonable period of time.
4. The system is still the same. The trading opportunities still exist. The signal patterns programmed into the model still exist in the data and precede the trades. The system is healthy and in good synchronization.

Holding Period Tolerance

Assume you are trading a system, it has an open long position that was initiated from a Buy signal, and the price of your issue is falling.

Is there some level of drawdown in your account equity that would cause you to not take the next trade? Or, more seriously, that would cause you to exit the open trade without waiting for the system exit?

What is the period of time you are willing to hold through without taking a subjective action? Five minutes, one hour, one day, one week? Or is it independent of a specific period of time? Can you always wait until the system issues the exit?

Trade Exits

The answers depend in part on how your system exits trades.

However a new position has been opened, there are five general ways to exit.
* Logic—trading system rules that issue a Sell signal.
* Maximum holding period, including inactivity.
* Profit target.
* Trailing exit.
* Maximum loss exit.

The system must have at least one of these, and it may have as many as all five. The exit prices may be set at entry and left unchanged for the entire trade, or they may be adjusted intra-trade.

One of the definitive aspects of using a quantitative system is that all of the rules are in the system. There are no external rules, either objective or subjective. When the system issues a Buy, a long position is taken, and it is held until the system issues a Sell.

In order to apply the pattern recognition, risk control, and position sizing techniques described in this book and my other materials, the answer to "what is the period of time you are willing to hold through?" must be "until the system issues the exit." What does that imply?

Since drawdown can increase rapidly over a multi-day market decline, that period must be short enough that price changes, including drawdown, within it can be ignored. The system will always hold through a period at least this long. I recommend the period between potential changes to position be no longer than one trading day. (Any shorter period, such as hourly, will work equally well providing intra-day data with appropriate bar lengths are used. To avoid awkward sentence construction, please interpret "daily" to mean "daily or more frequently" unless otherwise stated.)

Establishing the basic period as daily does not restrict entry and / or exit from occurring intra-day. End-of-day traders are able to use limit and stop orders to enter or exit at an intra-day price. However, with bars of any length, the inability to resolve intra-bar price action limits the number of potential trades in a single bar to the open, the close, and at most one intra-bar trade.

Manage Weekly?

If you are considering managing less frequently than daily, consider the following scenario.

You are managing weekly—updating data and checking for new signals over the weekend for possible action on Monday. Your risk tolerance is a maximum drawdown of 20%.

Today is Wednesday. The system entered the week with a 15% drawdown. The past three days have been volatile, the drawdown is now 23%, and indications are for a further price drop.

Having rules in place that you will wait for the system to signal the exit is causing some anxiety. Prudence suggests you should exit the trade. Of course, you have the ability to override the rules and enter the sell order. But augmenting the rule-based system with discretionary actions, no matter how or why they were taken, distorts the analysis of risk.

Futures traders have to consider another actor—the broker, margin clerk, and clearing agency. They will close your position as soon as their capital is at risk. Usually waiting until the close of trading, but inquire to be certain.

My point is that managing a trading account less frequently than daily may increase risk in ways that were not anticipated.

Maximum Adverse Excursion (MAE)

Maximum adverse excursion is a measure of the most unfavorable point in a trade, or in a period of time. MAE can be expressed as a positive number or negative; in points, dollars, or percentage. By convention we will express MAE as a positive number, and in whatever unit is appropriate. We want MAE to be small.

MAE is a measure of the risk we acknowledge.

For clarity, I refer to a bar as a day. The analysis and discussion applies equally well to bars of any length, and also to trades treated as bars.

Maximum Favorable Excursion (MFE)

Similar to MAE, maximum favorable excursion records the most favorable price. In a long trade, it is the highest high. When using mark-to-market, whenever there is a new MFE and it establishes a new high for the account equity, adjust the equity to reflect that gain.

If you subscribe to the idea that there are *two* absorbing boundaries—success and failure—a new maximum equity may cause you to stop trading because you have *gained enough*.

Accumulated MAE (AMAE)

Every trade has its own MAE, computed and reported daily. The accumulated drawdown spans trades and measures the highest marked-to-market bankable equity to lowest marked-to-market equity.

AMAE is the drawdown we use to measure risk.

Your goal in trading the system is to determine the proper maximum safe position size, on a trade-by-trade basis, so that the AMAE rarely exceeds your risk tolerance.

Bad Stuff Can Happen

In spite of your best system development efforts, there might be—probably will be—situations where a larger loss than the system—or you—anticipated occurred, but there are still open trades.

Management and measurement should coincide.

If it is necessary to do so, your action to declare the system broken, override the rules, exit open positions, and take the system offline should coincide with a point in time or in the trade where drawdown is measured. That is the point at which trades are marked-to-market.

If the intra-day drawdown is too severe, use shorter bars and mark-to-market after each bar. Or choose a less volatile issue to trade.

Your measurement period must agree with your management period.

Does intra-trade drawdown matter?

Yes. Consider the Will Rogers system.

> *Don't gamble; take all your savings and buy some good stock and hold it till it goes up, then sell it. If it don't go up, don't buy it.*

Written as a trading system, that might be:

```
Buy when the price rises above its 100 day moving average
Sell when there is a 5% profit
```

Figure 2.3 shows the equity curve, based on closed trades, for trading SPY using that system beginning in 1999. During periods spanning years 2000 to 2007 and 2008 to 2013—the long horizontal lines—there is an open position that is in a drawdown while you wait for the 5% profit.

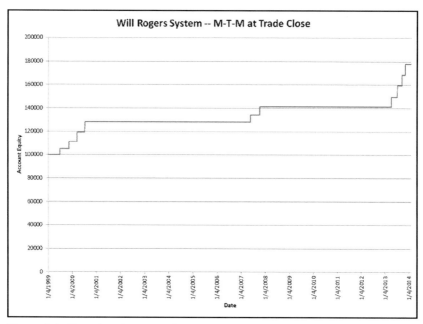

Figure 2.3 Closed trade equity for Will Rogers system

Figure 2.4 shows the equity curve with daily account balance changes. The two major drawdowns that you would be holding through are 45% and 55%.

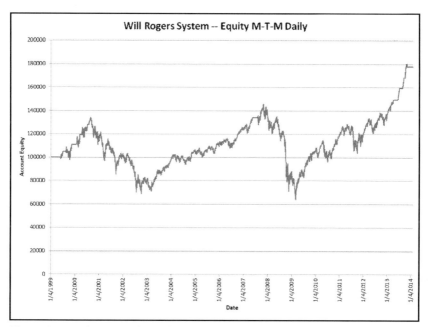

Figure 2.4 Daily equity for Will Rogers system

Imagine if the system had been trading Enron rather than SPY.

Mark-to-Market Equivalence

Figure 2.5 shows a table representing three multi-day trades. Entry to a long position is made at the close of the first day, at the closing price. Exit is at the close of the final day, at the closing price. The column headed "Trade" gives the gain of that trade—exit price divided by entry price. "Trade Sequence" gives the cumulative gain for the trade sequence. "Daily Change" is the day-by-day percentage change from the previous day. "Daily Cumulative" is the cumulative gain for the sequence of days within each trade. Note agreement between "Trade" and "Daily Cumulative" at the end of each trade. "Daily Sequence" is the cumulative gain for the sequence of days for the entire three trade sequence. Note the agreement between "Trade Sequence" and "Daily Sequence" at the end of the trade sequence.

	Daily price SPY Close	Trade	Trade Sequence	Daily Change	Daily Cumulative	Daily Sequence
4/11/2002	110.59 buy		1		1	1
4/12/2002	111.42			1.0075	1.0075	1.0075
4/15/2002	110.57			0.9924	0.9998	0.9998
4/16/2002	113.20			1.0238	1.0236	1.0236
4/17/2002	112.96			0.9979	1.0214	1.0214
4/18/2002	112.47			0.9957	1.0170	1.0170
4/19/2002	112.88 sell	1.0207	1.0207	1.0036	1.0207	1.0207
4/26/2002	107.39 buy				1	
4/29/2002	106.86			0.9951	0.9951	1.0157
4/30/2002	107.86			1.0094	1.0044	1.0252
5/1/2002	109.18			1.0122	1.0167	1.0377
5/2/2002	108.76 sell	1.0128	1.0337	0.9962	1.0128	1.0337
5/8/2002	109.01 buy				1	
5/9/2002	107.75			0.9884	0.9884	1.0218
5/10/2002	105.72 sell	0.9698	1.0025	0.9812	0.9698	1.0025

Figure 2.5 Equity change by trade and by day

From a mathematical perspective, the net equity change from a sequence of trades is identical whether the trades are considered as complete trades or as sequences of marked-to-market days.

From a trading management perspective, marking-to-market daily gives finer resolution to the performance of the system and the opportunity to make intra-trade subjective trading decisions, should they become necessary.

From a trading system design perspective, marking-to-market daily transforms every system, no matter how often it buys and sells, into a system that has 252 daily results every year. This reduces distortion that occurs at the start and end of every evaluation period. It also increases the number of data points available for trade selection, and entry and exit signals.

Converting from impulse signals to state signals provides the opportunity for better measurement and better management. State signals are discussed in more detail in Chapter 3.

Although the trades extend over multiple days, the system design and system management focus is on the mark-to-market period—daily.

This does not imply changing positions every day. It does imply evaluating every day, and willingness to change positions daily. It allows us to ask the questions "What is the distribution of next day return?" and "Should the position for the next day be long, flat, or short?"

In terms of changes to account equity and drawdown, an n-day trade is equivalent to n one-day trades.

Quantifying Risk Tolerance

Recall the discussion of risk tolerance from Chapter 1. Every trader or trading company has a level of risk tolerance. It is the level of drawdown that, when exceeded, causes the trader to accept that the system is broken and must be taken offline. Risk tolerance can be quantified.

Repeating the risk tolerance statement introduced in Chapter 1:

> I am trading a $100,000 account and looking forward two years. I am willing to accept a 5% risk of a 20% drawdown, measured from highest equity to date.

It has four parameters:
• Account size.
• Forecast horizon.
• Maximum drawdown.
• Degree of certainty.

Account Size

The initial balance of the trading account at the beginning of the period. With the understanding that the utility of money is an important issue, it is ignored here. But, needing specific numbers for examples, the initial balance is set at $100,000. Adjust to reflect your trading.

Since we are measuring in percentage changes, it is not a critical issue at this point.

Forecast Horizon

The depth of a drawdown sometime in the future depends on how far into the future we look. Pick a length of time that fits your business plan and trading activity. We call this the *forecast horizon*. It will be set to two years for these examples. Both estimates of future drawdowns and realized drawdowns increase as the length of the forecast horizon is increased. Think of the oft-quoted, and accurate, warning that "your greatest drawdown lies in the future."

Maximum Drawdown

The trader's risk tolerance is the drawdown at which the system is taken offline in recognition that it is not working as expected. As we will see, account growth, position size, and drawdown are linked. Being too conservative on maximum drawdown limits account growth. Being too liberal increases the probability of a steep drawdown and the difficulty of recovering from it. Individual traders might be willing to accept 20%.

Select this value carefully. Your system has a positive expectation. For a given number of trades, increasing position size increases account growth. Increasing position size also increases drawdown. The dynamic position sizing and safe-f technique will limit drawdown to your tolerance, black swan events excepted. But it will keep position size as high as is safe for as long as it is safe. The drawdowns realized in trading will reach your tolerance. If you specify that you can tolerate a 20% drawdown, you will experience a 20% drawdown.

Money managers who prefer to hold drawdowns to single digits and have no losing years might use 10% or less instead of 20%. Use whatever level you are comfortable with.

As we will see in a section below, risk increases as holding period increases. Traders preferring longer holding periods must be prepared to either accept higher risk or trade at a smaller position size.

Degree of Certainty

We seldom get opportunities to recover from serious mistakes, so we should reduce the chances of having even one drawdown as severe as the limit we have chosen. If one chance in twenty sounds about right, that is a 5% chance. 5% corresponds well with our understanding of statistical significance. We say that an event is *significant* at the 5% level.

A Chart Illustrating Risk Tolerance

Good! We have a well defined statement of risk tolerance. We know enough to draw a picture illustrating the risk tolerance. Figure 2.6 shows the cumulative distribution function (CDF) of drawdown for a simple trading system. The circle at the right edge of the page identifies the risk tolerance of the example statement on the previous page—a 5% chance of a 20% maximum drawdown. The next few sections describe how to create this chart from a set of trades.

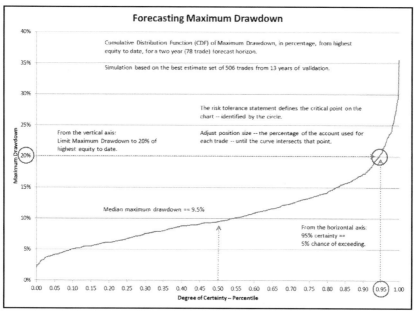

Figure 2.6 Chart illustrating a statement of risk tolerance

This chart was produced using a Monte Carlo simulation. A trading system was designed, coded, and tested using daily end-of-day data for the period 1/1/1999 through 1/1/2012. Validation produced a set of 506 trades for the 13 year period. That set of trades was used as the *best estimate* of future performance. Assuming that future performance is similar to that of the best estimate, a two-year forecast horizon will have about 78 trades. A Monte Carlo simulation was coded in Excel using the techniques described in my Modeling book.[1]

The fixed fraction technique was used for position sizing. The fraction of the account used for each trade that produced this curve is 63%. This means that whenever a Buy signal is generated by the system, buy as many shares as possible using 63% of the current balance of the trading account. That value, 63%, was determined by an iterative search. The fraction was adjusted in order to find the value where there was a 5% chance that the maximum drawdown would exceed 20%. That is, to find the fraction where the CDF curve passed through the point defining the statement of risk tolerance.

---

1   Bandy, Howard, *Modeling Trading System Performance*, Blue Owl Press, 2011.

The resulting cumulative distribution function of percentage maximum drawdown is plotted in Figure 2.6. The 5% certainty comes from the horizontal axis, where the 95th percentile corresponds to a 5% chance of a greater drawdown. The 20% maximum drawdown comes from the vertical axis.

Tail Risk and Black Swans

We can estimate the *tail risk*—the depth of the worst drawdown—by observing the extreme right side of the distribution—the area above the 95th percentile. The extreme tail risk for Figure 2.6 is 36%. Black swans live and hide in the tail of the distribution.

Producing the CDF for Estimate of Risk

The histogram in Figure 2.7 shows a probability mass function (pmf). A pmf is for discrete data what a probability density function (pdf) is for continuous data. The maximum drawdown from each of the 1000 simulation runs described above was recorded, then sorted into bins 0.5% wide. The heights of the histogram bars show the proportion of drawdowns in each of the respective bins. For an interpretation, consider the tallest histogram bar—the bin at 9%, is 6.3% high. That means that of the 1000 simulation runs, 6.3%, or 63, of them had a maximum drawdown between 8.75% and 9.25%. (Since the bins are each 0.5% wide, the 9% bin includes 8.75% to 9.25%.)

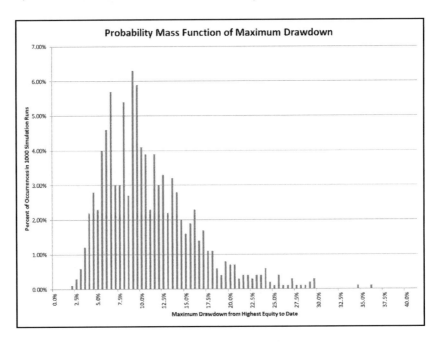

Figure 2.7 Probability mass function of maximum drawdown

The CDF is more useful for our purposes. To form the CDF, beginning at the leftmost bin of the histogram of the pmf, compute the running sum of percentages. CDFs always have a range of 0.0 to 1.0. The resulting CDF is shown in Figure 2.8.

Figures 2.6 and 2.8 show the same data, but with the axes exchanged. In Figure 2.6, the percentile scale is on the horizontal axis, and the function is more properly called the *inverse CDF*. Most of the CDFs we will work with are displayed like Figure 2.6 and are inverse CDFs. Since there will likely be no confusion, either format of the function will be referred to as a CDF.

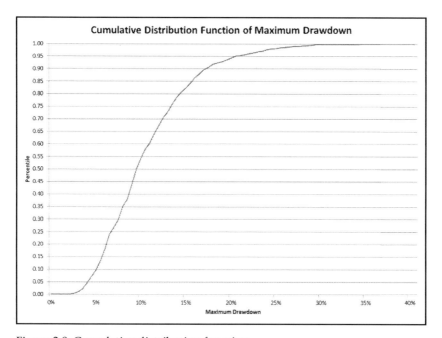

Figure 2.8 Cumulative distribution function

Backtest Equity Curve

For interest, Figure 2.9 shows the equity curve for the validation trades for the system. There is no compounding or other position sizing—each trade is the number of shares that can be purchased by the same dollar amount. This is about as benign, smooth, and safe looking an equity curve as ever results from an out-of-sample test.

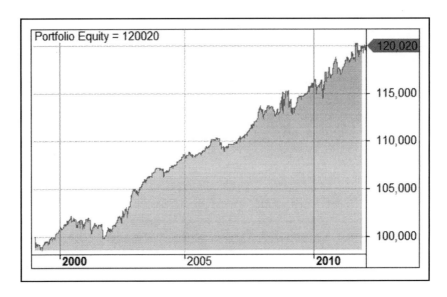

Figure 2.9 Equity curve for example system

Trade at Full Fraction

Yet, this system can only be traded at a fraction of 0.63 without risk exceeding the desired limits. If all funds were used for each trade— trading the system at a fraction of 1.00, or *full fraction*—the risk rises considerably, as the CDF in Figure 2.10 shows. Figures 2.6 and 2.10 use the same scales. The change in position of the CDF curve illustrates the change in risk. Changing from fraction, f, of 0.63 (shown in Figure 2.6) to f of 1.00 (shown in Figure 2.10) raises the CDF curve as the risk is raised. If the certainty remains at 5%, maximum drawdown increases from 20% to 30%—the tail of large drawdowns increases. Alternatively, if the maximum drawdown remains at 20%, the certainty drops from 5% to 25%—from a 1 in 20 chance to a 1 in 4 chance of a 20% drawdown. Not shown because it is truncated by the scale limitation, extreme tail risk when traded at full fraction rises to more than 48%.

To be clear—the funds used to trade this system are exposed to the drawdown shown in Figure 2.10. There is a 25% chance of a 20% drawdown, and a 5% chance of a 30% drawdown, in those funds. That is a characteristic of the system. You cannot change that.

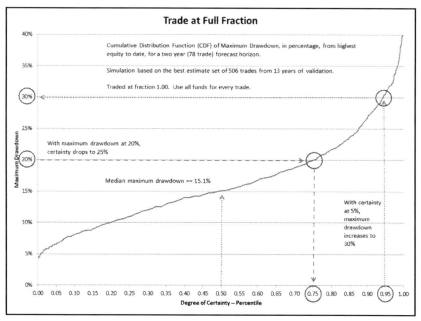

Figure 2.10 CDF of maximum drawdown traded at full fraction

Allocate a Portion to Risk Free

What you can do is place a portion of the funds you allocate to this system in a risk-free account to act as ballast. The 63% will have draw-downs greater than your tolerance. The combination of traded funds plus ballast funds will have drawdowns limited to your tolerance.

Consider trading this system for two years—a hypothetical example.

Initial account balance is $100,000. Final balance after two years is $121,000, using safe-f of 0.63. The $100,000 is divided into $37,000 which is placed in a risk-free account at the start of trading, and $63,000 used to trade the system. The account gains, loses, and recovers to finish higher. It is measured at four times—initial, highest equity, lowest equity, final.

Equity				
	Initial	Highest	Lowest	Final
Ballast	37,000	37,000	37,000	37,000
Trading	63,000	70,000	50,000	84,000
Total	100,000	107,000	87,000	121,000

Figure 2.11 Balance of the two components

The bar chart in Figure 2.12 shows the relative balance of each of the two components.

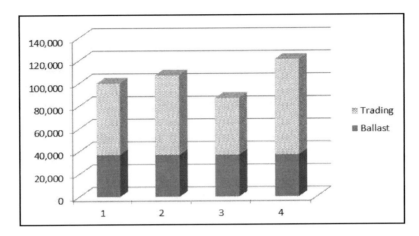

Figure 2.12 Relative balance of the two components

The drawdown in the trading component from $70,000 to $50,000 is 29%. The drawdown in the account, including the ballast funds, from $107,000 to $87,000 is 19%.

Estimating Profit Potential

Just as drawdown is a distribution, profit is a distribution. When the position size is set to 0.63, the value of safe-f, and the Monte Carlo simulation is repeated, the percentage gain (final equity divided by initial equity—TWR in Ralph Vince's terminology) of each run is computed. Together, these 1000 runs form a pmf similar to the one in Figure 2.7. A CDF, similar to the one in Figure 2.6, is also formed—this one is of final equity. See Figure 2.13.

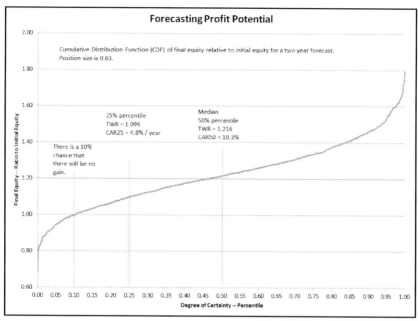

Figure 2.13 CDF of final equity

The horizontal axis is the degree of certainty measured in percentage. The 0.25 mark represents the 25th percentile, the 0.50 mark is the median. The curve is the CDF of final equity.

The area at the left side where the CDF is less than 1.0 shows the probability there will be no profit over a two year period. It is about 10%. There is a 1 in 10 chance that trading this system for two years, even managing position size conservatively using dynamic position sizing and safe-f, will lose money.

The median TWR is 1.216, which corresponds to a compound annual rate of return (CAR) of 10.3%.

I have selected the 25th percentile as the metric of profit potential. Call it CAR25. CAR25 for this system is 4.8% per year. There is a three out of four chance that annual growth will exceed 4.8%.

CAR25 is the risk-normalized profit potential for the trading system tested. Its value for this system is 4.8%. If there are other opportunities to use these funds, prefer the one with the highest CAR25.

Sidebar—Calculating CAR

Terminal wealth relative, TWR, is the term coined by Ralph Vince to represent the ratio of final equity to initial equity. In terms of the simulation, TWR is EqAtClose / initial equity. Final equity (TWR), compound annual rate of return (CAR), and number of years (N), are related by these formulas:

$$TWR = (1+CAR)^N$$

$$CAR = exp(ln(TWR)/N) - 1$$

For a two year forecast period, a close approximation of CAR, expressed as a percent, is given by:

$$CAR = 100.0 * (sqrt(TWR) - 1)$$

For example, if an account grows from $100,000 to $115,000 in two years, TWR is 1.15. The corresponding compound annual rate of growth is 7.2%

Trade Quality

We periodically read articles that recommend holding long positions for long periods of time. The argument revolves around an analysis of equity gain related to missing a very few of the best days in a period, suggesting it is essential to remain invested in order to benefit from those few special days. Since this is a book about trading system development, and we are looking for alternatives to buy and hold that provide for account growth while avoiding large drawdowns, we can answer the best day versus worst day question using the techniques just described—compare profit potential on a risk-normalized basis.

Example System

We begin with a trading system based on the 2 period RSI of closing price as an indicator. Call it RSI2. The system enters a long position when RSI2 falls through a level of 36, and exits when RSI2 rises through a level of 36. The system was tested on several major equity index ETFs for the 13 year period of 1999 through 2011. Figure 2.14 shows the equity curve for one of the issues.

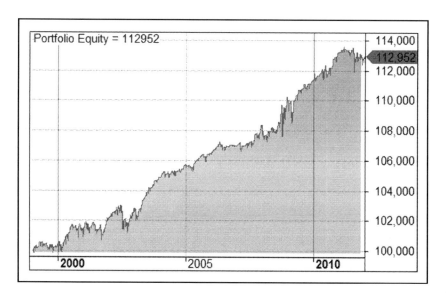

Figure 2.14 Equity curve for constant size trades

Figure 2.15 shows the statistics. There are 517 trades, each of which gains about 0.25%, on average. The summary report in Figure 2.15 shows average bars held to be 3.22. The development program counts the entry day. For this system, there is no equity change on entry day, so we will not count it as one of the holding period days, making the average holding period 2.22 days. Trade accuracy is about 71%. On average, losing trades are held longer than winning trades, and the magnitude of the average loss is greater than of the average win.

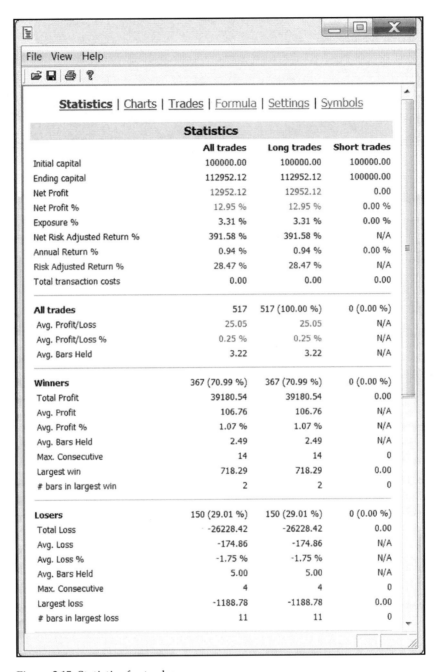

Figure 2.15 Statistics for trades

Figure 2.16 shows the 517 trades, sorted by gain.

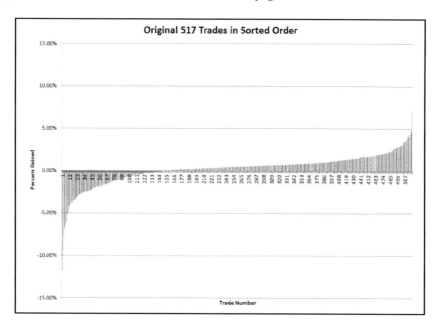

Figure 2.16 Trades in sorted order

The by-now-familiar simulation is used to compute safe-f for a risk tolerance of 5% / 20% / 2 years. It turns out to be 0.883, and the interquartile CAR values are CAR25 = 3.4% and CAR75 = 14.3%.

To study how the best trades and the worst trades affect performance, we will analyze four more sets of trades. Each simulation run begins with the same 517 trades, then modified by adding or removing five percent (26) winning trades or losing trades. The five simulations are:

A. The original 517 trades.
B. Add winners. Copy the best 26 trades and add them to the trade list, resulting in 543 trades.
C. Add losers. Copy the worst 26 trades and add them to the trade list.
D. Remove winners. Remove the 26 best trades from the list, resulting in 491 trades.
E. Remove losers. Remove the 26 worst trades from the list.

Five simulation runs were made, each trading full fraction. The five CDFs of maximum drawdown are shown in Figure 2.17.

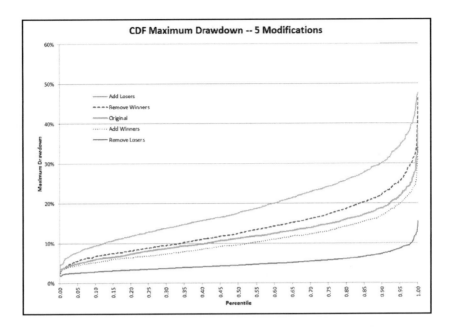

Figure 2.17 CDFs of maximum drawdown for modified trade list

We prefer systems with lower drawdown—those lower on the chart. The uppermost curve is the one where losing trades were added. Increasing losing trades increases drawdown. The lowermost curve is the one where losing trades were removed. Decreasing losing trades decreases drawdown. The curves where winners were either added or removed—just above and below the middle curve—did not change the result as much.

Losing trades are clearly more important than winning trades in determining risk.

Limitation to any trading system is the number and magnitude of losing trades. When there are large losing trades, or when losing trades occur close together in sequence, the result is large drawdowns.

Recall that safe-f is computed so that the risk of a 20% drawdown is 5%. We can describe this as *normalizing for risk*. When normalized for risk, the profit potential of alternative trading systems can be compared directly.

Safe-f was determined for each of the five sets of trades, normalizing the drawdown at the 95th percentile, and the profit potential of each was computed. The safe-f values, in A, B, C, D, E order, were 0.88, 1.01, 0.55, 0.72, and 2.53. Figure 2.18 shows the five CDFs of final equity when each is traded at its safe-f position size. Higher is better. Note the significantly higher profit for the trade list that had the worst five percent of trades removed.

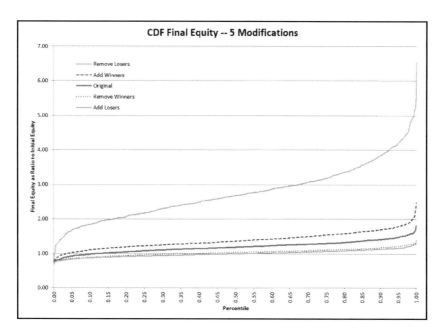

Figure 2.18 CDFs of profit potential

While it would be ideal to remove only the worst trades, that will be difficult. Figure 2.19 shows an interesting comparison where both the five percent best trades and the five percent worst trades have been removed. Normalized for risk, performance is significantly better for the set of trades that do not include the losing trades. There is less risk of having a loss at the end of the two year period, and CAR is higher across the distribution.

Even at the expense of missing good trades, it is important to avoid bad trades.

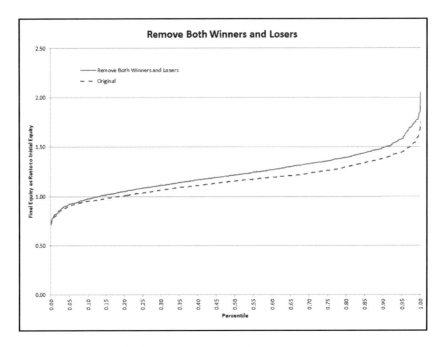

Figure 2.19 Remove both best and worst trades

Market Research

Market research is a natural part of a business plan. If you were considering starting a company to sell running shoes, you would do some market research. You would find out how many potential customers there were and how much profit there was in each pair sold. There is no guarantee your product would be successful. Developing a good product line and selling are yet to come. But you would be unwise to start if you knew there was no market or the profit margin was too low.

Or perhaps you have a case of gold fever. Is there gold in those hills over there? How much? How hard to extract? Before buying the property and bringing in the heavy equipment, let's send in a prospector.

Blue Owl Prospecting, Inc.

Let us dig around in your data.

We will identify the risks and estimate the profit potential. We will tell you how accurate your system must be. Then you can decide which issues have the best prospects and begin developing those systems.

There is an analogy with trading systems. The best issues to trade combine three characteristics:
* Adequate profit potential—some price variation.
* Absence of extreme adverse price changes—not too much price variation.
* Existence of detectable signal patterns—not too efficient.

Goldilocks, to be sure.

Additionally, the issue must be sufficiently liquid. I recommend enough liquidity so you can exit your entire position any minute of any day without substantially affecting the bid-ask spread.

The complete trading system consists of the model and the data series. Even before we begin model development, we can determine how much profit is potentially available by analyzing the data series itself.

Risk and Profit Potential

There is quantifiable risk inherent in any data series. Whatever system is eventually developed to trade it, some trades will be winners and some will be losers. All trades, winners as well as losers, have adverse excursions that contribute to the drawdown.

Given a data series and two variables—holding period and system accuracy—we can estimate the risk inherent in the series. Given the risk inherent in the series and your personal statement of risk tolerance, we can determine safe-f. Given safe-f, we can estimate profit potential.

The analysis described here assumes:
* You have a trading system that trades a single issue and is either long or flat.
* All the rules have been included in the model.
* There will be no subjective position changes or early exits.
* Equity is marked-to-market at the close of every trading day.

Simulation Outline

The analysis is done using a Monte Carlo simulator implemented in a Python program.

We are choosing trades that total two years of long exposure, however many trades that requires and however much time that covers. Imagine you are alternately long and flat, then squeeze out the flat periods, resulting in two years of long trades.

The major control variables are:
- Your risk tolerance. Say a maximum 5% chance of a drawdown greater than 20% over a 2 year horizon.
- The issue being tested. Say SPY. The simulator is set up for daily data. Closing prices are required. If daily high and low are present, they can be used.
- Any time period longer than the forecast period can be used. The ideal is what is representative of the future. Within reason, longer is better. Say 1999 through 2014.
- The holding period of each trade in days. Any value up to the length of the forecast is valid. Say 5 days.
- Accuracy of the trading system. Any value from 0.00 (every trade is a loser) to 1.00 (every trade is a winner) can be used. Say 65%, represented as 0.65.
- The number of simulation runs. Say 1000.

The simulation works as follows.

Preliminaries.
1. Set the control variables.
2. Select a daily price series.
3. Given the holding period, examine every day as an entry day. Positions will be taken market on close, at the closing price. Look ahead the number of days of the holding period. That will be the exit day. If the closing price on the exit day is higher, mark this entry day as a "gainer" entry day; otherwise it is a "loser" entry day.
4. Divide the number of days in the forecast period by the holding period, giving the number of trades.
5. Set the fraction used for each trade to 1.00.

For each of the required number of simulation runs, repeat the following sequence for as many trades as are needed to complete the forecast horizon:
1. Pick a random number (uniform, 0.00 to 1.00) to determine whether the next trade will be a winner or a loser. Over the course of many runs, the proportion of winning trades matches the trade accuracy you want to study.

2. From whichever list—"gainer" or "loser"—was chosen, select a trade entry day at random. Note the entry price. Buy as many shares as you can with the fraction of equity allowed.
3. In the sequence that they occur in the historical price series, process the trade day-by-day. Keep daily track of:
    * Intra-day drawdown, measured using daily high and low.
    * Intra-trade drawdown, measured using mark-to-market daily closing price.
    * Trade drawdown, measured from the trade open to trade close.
    * Account equity—value of shares held plus cash.

At the completion of those trades, the simulator reports the three drawdown metrics and the final equity.

Figure 2.20 shows ten equally likely equity curves resulting from trading SPY with a holding period of 5 days, an accuracy of 65%, and a fraction of 1.00.

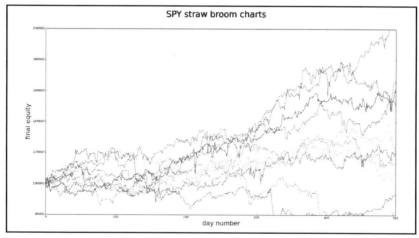

Figure 2.20 Equity, two years of SPY, fraction 1.00

Figure 2.21 shows a table with the metrics for those ten runs. The first few lines of output document the values of the control variables. Not shown, initial equity is $100,000.

There is one row for each run. Interpretation of the columns, using the first row as an example, is:
* Max IDDD is the maximum intra-day drawdown over the two year period. The value in the first run is 0.3620, meaning there was a 36.2% drawdown in equity measured from highest daily high price to date to a subsequent daily low price.
* Max ITDD is the maximum intra-trade drawdown. The first run had a drawdown of 34.09% using mark-to-market closing prices. This is the metric we wish to hold to 20%.

- Max TRDD is the maximum trade-by-trade drawdown—33.3%. This is the drawdown using only the sequence of 100 5-day trades, ignoring all intra-trade price variation.
- EqAtClose is the final equity—$93,285.
- CAR is the compound annual rate of return—a loss of 3.42% per year.

```
Issue: spy
Dates: 01 Jan 1999 to: 01 Jan 2015
Hold Days: 5
System Accuracy:  0.650000
DD 95 limit: 0.200000
Fraction: 1.000000
Forecast Horizon: 504
Number Forecasts: 10
Max IDDD: 0.3620    Max ITDD: 0.3409    Max TRDD: 0.3330    EqAtClose: 93285     CAR: -3.42
Max IDDD: 0.1689    Max ITDD: 0.1573    Max TRDD: 0.1434    EqAtClose: 113211    CAR: 6.40
Max IDDD: 0.1399    Max ITDD: 0.1206    Max TRDD: 0.0855    EqAtClose: 208173    CAR: 44.28
Max IDDD: 0.1410    Max ITDD: 0.1345    Max TRDD: 0.0928    EqAtClose: 125937    CAR: 12.22
Max IDDD: 0.1635    Max ITDD: 0.1379    Max TRDD: 0.1184    EqAtClose: 151131    CAR: 22.94
Max IDDD: 0.2075    Max ITDD: 0.2032    Max TRDD: 0.1713    EqAtClose: 107548    CAR: 3.71
Max IDDD: 0.1477    Max ITDD: 0.1336    Max TRDD: 0.0743    EqAtClose: 162239    CAR: 27.37
Max IDDD: 0.2600    Max ITDD: 0.2499    Max TRDD: 0.2263    EqAtClose: 120118    CAR: 9.60
Max IDDD: 0.3941    Max ITDD: 0.3852    Max TRDD: 0.3696    EqAtClose: 75432     CAR: -13.15
Max IDDD: 0.1607    Max ITDD: 0.1484    Max TRDD: 0.1345    EqAtClose: 164959    CAR: 28.44
```

Figure 2.21 Metrics for the ten equity curves

The risk tolerance requires intra-trade marked-to-market daily drawdown at the 95th percentile to be no greater than 20 percent. Intra-trade marked-to-market-daily drawdown is the second column—Max ITDD. If results for all 1000 runs were listed and sorted by that column, we want the first 950 to have values less than 0.2000, the final 50 to be greater. There is no advantage in having the final 50 be less than 0.2000, a situation that would occur only if the fraction of available equity used for each trade was lower than the maximum safe-f. Intentionally using a lower fraction does lower risk, but it also lowers profit. You do want to coordinate your risk tolerance with the fraction used and take the largest positions that are safe.

Note that four of the ten runs shown in Figure 2.21 have values greater than 0.2000. This combination—5 day holding with 65% accuracy—is too risky when traded at full fraction.

This does not mean that a system that is 65% accurate and holds trades five days cannot be profitably traded. It does mean that, in order to avoid unacceptable drawdowns, only a fraction of the available funds can be safely used. The remainder must remain in a risk free account to act as a ballast.

What is the largest that fraction should be? The metrics shown in Figures 2.20 and 2.21 result from taking every trade with all available funds—fraction of 1.00. The 95th percentile maximum intra-trade drawdown for all 1000 runs was 30.1 percent.

The simulation searches for the highest fraction for which the metric Max ITDD is 0.20 or less in 95% of the runs. That is safe-f for this issue, holding period, and accuracy. Safe-f is found to be 0.646.

We know that position size is not stationary. Safe-f varies over time as the characteristics of the data change. For now, using an assumption of stationarity considerably simplifies the analysis and explanation.

Figure 2.22 shows ten equally likely equity curves for the same holding period and accuracy as those shown in Figure 2.20, but with a fraction of 0.646 rather than 1.00.

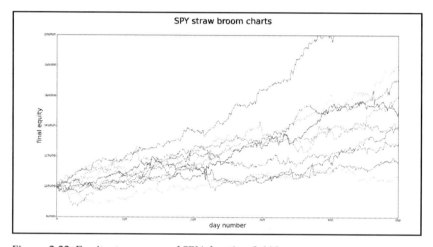

Figure 2.22 Equity, two years of SPY, fraction 0.646

Figure 2.23 shows the associated table.

```
Issue: spy
Dates: 01 Jan 1999 to: 01 Jan 2015
Hold Days: 5
System Accuracy:  0.650000
DD 95 limit: 0.200000
Fraction: 0.646000
Forecast Horizon: 504
Number Forecasts: 10
Max IDDD: 0.1223    Max ITDD: 0.1010    Max TRDD: 0.0728    EqAtClose: 138520    CAR: 17.69
Max IDDD: 0.1271    Max ITDD: 0.1157    Max TRDD: 0.0917    EqAtClose: 137760    CAR: 17.37
Max IDDD: 0.1998    Max ITDD: 0.1667    Max TRDD: 0.1286    EqAtClose: 115721    CAR: 7.57
Max IDDD: 0.0962    Max ITDD: 0.0837    Max TRDD: 0.0773    EqAtClose: 179749    CAR: 34.07
Max IDDD: 0.1025    Max ITDD: 0.0941    Max TRDD: 0.0882    EqAtClose: 128546    CAR: 13.38
Max IDDD: 0.1225    Max ITDD: 0.1155    Max TRDD: 0.1086    EqAtClose: 107178    CAR: 3.53
Max IDDD: 0.1589    Max ITDD: 0.1275    Max TRDD: 0.0811    EqAtClose: 149333    CAR: 22.20
Max IDDD: 0.0818    Max ITDD: 0.0759    Max TRDD: 0.0672    EqAtClose: 228167    CAR: 51.05
Max IDDD: 0.1549    Max ITDD: 0.1492    Max TRDD: 0.0958    EqAtClose: 159437    CAR: 26.27
Max IDDD: 0.1355    Max ITDD: 0.1310    Max TRDD: 0.1230    EqAtClose: 170265    CAR: 30.49
```

Figure 2.23 Metrics for the ten equity curves

Drawdown as a Function of Holding Period

Continuing to use SPY as the issue, set fraction to 1.00, and use the 5% / 20% / 2 year statement of risk tolerance. Run a series of simulations. Begin with trade accuracy at 50%, then 55, 60, 65, 70, 80, and 90. For each of the seven levels of trade accuracy, vary the holding period from 1 day to 252 days. Record the value of ITDD95—the 95th percentile intra-trade drawdown. This is the number you want to hold to 20% or less.

Figure 2.24 shows the relationship between drawdown and holding period and accuracy. The horizontal axis is holding period in days; the vertical axis is maximum drawdown in percent; the dashed horizontal line at 20% is your risk tolerance. Each of the lines with dots represents one of the levels of trade accuracy. The 50% level is closest to the top of the chart, progressing downward with 90% accuracy the lowest line. On this chart, lower is better. The circled dot is 65% accurate, 5 day hold—the values analyzed in detail in the preceding sections. Sharp-eyed readers will note the circled value is slightly less than 30%, while the figure given for safe-f earlier was 30.1%. Variations of this sort are to be expected when working with Monte Carlo simulations.

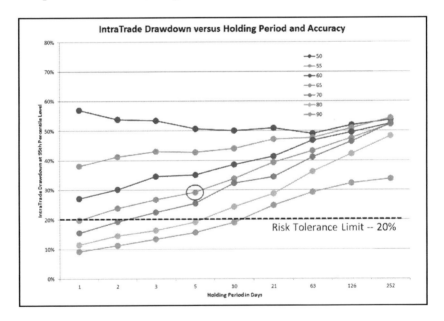

Figure 2.24 Drawdown related to holding period and accuracy

Figure 2.24 shows that the maximum safe position size decreases as holding period increases, and it decreases as accuracy decreases.

Drawdown increases as holding period increases.

Drawdown increases as trade accuracy decreases.

This does not mean systems that hold longer than 5 days or have accuracy less than 70% cannot be profitable. It does mean they cannot be traded at full fraction.

Only those combinations of trade accuracy and holding period plotted below the 20% drawdown limit can be traded at full fraction. To get a very rough estimate of the fraction that is safe for any combination of holding period and trade accuracy, locate that point on the graph, note the corresponding value of maximum drawdown from the vertical axis, and divide 0.20 by that value. For example, if your system is 60% accurate in selecting trades that hold one month (21 trading days), go up from 21 days to the 60% curve, then left to the axis, and read off the value of about 42%. 0.20 divided by 0.42 gives 0.48. The interpretation is that the maximum safe fraction for this system is to use 48% of available funds to buy shares, keeping the remaining 52% in cash. (Really in cash and really allocated solely to this system. These funds are not available to be used "twice" by also using them as the cash reserve for another system.) The relationship is not quite as linear as the simple division would suggest—the further above 0.20 the system is, the lower the safe fraction.

Profit Potential

When 65% accurate holding 5 days, maximum intra-trade drawdown is about 30%, and maximum safe fraction is about 64%. Given these parameters, we can estimate the potential profit. That is, trading SPY for two years of exposure, using a yet-to-be-defined model that results in trades that are held five days, of which 65 percent are winners, we can compute the distribution of final equity and associated compound annual rate of return (CAR). Figure 2.25 is that cumulative distribution function (CDF).

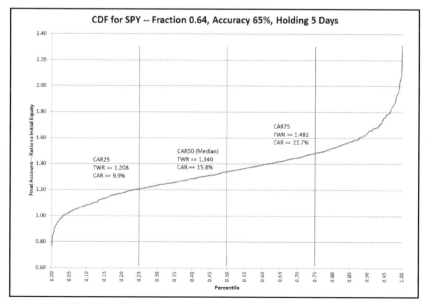

Figure 2.25 CDF for SPY

The CAR actually experienced will depend on the specific trades, but if the future resembles the past—where the past is 1999 to 2014 data—estimates can be read from the graph.

The 50th percentile is the median. The interquartile range is another useful metric. It is the difference between the values at the 25th percentile and those at the 75th percentile. Results are equally likely to be within this range as to be outside it to one extreme or the other.

For conciseness, these three will be called CAR25, CAR50, and CAR75. The results for SPY traded at a fraction of 64% are 9.9, 15.8, and 21.7.

It is typical for CAR75 to be about one and one-half to two times CAR25, with CAR50 about at their midpoint. Any large differences should be checked for unadjusted splits or data errors. In a few cases, CAR75 is much greater than typical. These are probably because of a few rapid prices rises.

Thus defined, profit potential is related to accuracy and holding period. As shown in Figure 2.26, profit potential increases as holding period is reduced and as trade accuracy is increased. The area outlined in the upper right corner contains those combinations where CAR25 is 10% or greater.

Compound Annual Rate of Return -- SPY -- Long Positions							
Accuracy							
Holding	40	50	55	60	65	70	80	90
1	-7.4	-2.6	5.9	28.0	74.0	161.0	725.0	3546.0
2	-6.4	-2.1	4.3	17.0	40.0	75.0	228.0	725.0
3	-6.4	-2.0	1.6	10.0	25.0	46.0	129.0	294.0
5	-5.4	-1.7	1.8	7.7	15.3	29.0	70.0	145.0
10	-4.6	-1.8	0.4	3.5	8.1	14.3	31.0	62.0
21	-3.7	-1.5	0.2	2.0	4.3	7.3	15.1	28.0
63	-2.0	-0.5	0.3	1.4	2.7	4.6	7.8	15.0
126	-1.6	-0.3	0.3	0.8	1.9	3.0	5.2	9.1
252	-1.7	-0.8	-0.5	-0.2	1.3	1.9	3.8	5.7

Figure 2.26 Median CAR versus Accuracy and Holding Period—Long

Note that the CAR figures reported in Figure 2.26 represent two years of holding a position. A system that is either long or flat would be long only a portion of that time, say, one-third. If so, it would take about six total years to accumulate two years of long exposure. Consequently, the reported CAR figures should be divided by three to estimate the maximum effective rate of return before the model is developed.

Risk in Being Short

We hear that being short is dangerous. That it is riskier than being long. We are told that the potential loss from a long stock position is "only" the amount lost when the price goes to zero, but the potential loss from a short position is unlimited because price has no upper limit.

The maximum drawdown for a long position is the entry price minus the lowest close of the holding period. The risk to a long position is a sharp price drop. The maximum drawdown for a short position is the highest close of the holding period minus the entry price. The risk to a short position is a sharp price rise.

Continuing with the same technique of estimating the risk inherent in a data series for a given holding period and trade accuracy, the maximum drawdown, safe-f, and median CAR is computed for short positions in SPY. If being short is indeed riskier, safe-f will be smaller, CAR will be lower, and the outlined area will be smaller.

The risk-normalized CAR25 for short positions is shown in Figure 2.27. These values are directly comparable with those for long positions in Figure 2.26.

Compound Annual Rate of Return -- SPY -- Short Positions								
Accuracy								
Holding	40	50	55	60	65	70	80	90
1	-6.1	2.2	22.2	59.0	142.0	252.0	825.0	12180.0
2	-5.4	2.2	13.4	32.2	72.0	128.0	256.0	797.0
3	-4.3	3.0	12.0	27.2	51.0	80.0	202.0	507.0
5	-4.1	1.1	6.3	15.6	27.3	44.0	102.0	203.0
10	-2.8	1.9	5.3	10.6	16.4	25.6	51.0	91.0
21	-2.6	1.6	4.0	8.8	11.9	16.3	32.9	51.0
63	-1.9	0.5	1.2	2.8	5.2	5.7	12.1	17.3
126	-2.0	0.9	-0.4	2.1	4.4	6.4	7.9	12.3
252	0.2	0.8	1.1	2.3	4.0	5.3	6.9	9.9

Figure 2.27 Median CAR versus Accuracy and Holding Period—Short

In both figures, the outlined area encloses those combinations that result in CAR25 greater than 10 percent. In every cell in the outlined area, CAR for a short position is higher than CAR for a long position.

There may be other reasons for not taking short positions, but riskiness is not one of them. Being short is inherently safer than being long.

This should come as no surprise. Research suggests and experience confirms that sharp drops in price are more common than sharp rises.

The outlined areas in Figures 2.26 and 2.27 contain those accuracy and holding period combinations that have a CAR25 of 10 percent or higher for a period of exposure of two years. This is the maximum potential inherent in the data for the given risk tolerance. We will not know what portion of this potential is achievable until a model is developed to detect patterns and trade this data series. Outside the outlined area, even with a trading system that captures all of the available profit, the return is equivalent to bank interest or less.

There is an implication that will make many people very uncomfortable.

Not only is the sweet spot highly accurate trade selection with a holding period of only a few days—but the further the system performance is away from the sweet spot area, the lower the possibility of a return greater than risk-free bank interest without experiencing drawdowns that will exceed your risk tolerance.

What the Prospector Found

The analysis described so far in this chapter has been for SPY. Expanding our analysis, we asked the Blue Owl Prospector to evaluate a variety of stocks and ETFs. We want to know what accuracy and holding period we might use with what data series.

Before spending the effort trying to develop a model to use with a data series, we want some assurance the resulting system has the possibility of satisfactory performance. Recall that we want a combination of:
- Enough variability to give opportunity for profitable trades.
- Enough stability that sharp price changes are infrequent.
- Enough history to assess performance in rising and falling markets.
- Enough liquidity to be able to exit a position easily.

We will pick issues to develop models from those that pass these screens.

Everything is in the context of a statement of personal risk tolerance. We are using 5% / 20% / 2 years.

The metrics we will examine and compare are:
- History. The most recent five years have been a strongly rising market. About eight years, 2000 days, of data will ensure both enough data points to give consistent simulation results and experience in a weak market. Plot every data series you are considering. Look for anomalies and correct any you find before beginning model development.
- CAR25 high enough to beat bank interest. CAR25 was chosen because it describes a lower limit for 75 percent of the distribution. For this analysis, we want a minimum CAR25 of 30. The long/flat or short/flat analysis is for two years of exposure. Assuming roughly equal periods of long, flat, and short, it will take six years of trading to get two years of exposure, a factor of three. So, divide 30 by three. We do not have a model yet. Some of the profit potential reported is random and cannot be predicted by any model. We do not know what portion that is, so let's assume a yet-to-be-developed model might capture half, a factor of two. So, divide

again—this time by two. Ideal CAR25 of 30 becomes potential CAR25 of 5—just high enough to compete with bank interest, or your risk-free alternative.

- Safe-f is the maximum fraction of the account that can be used to take positions. The remainder must be held in reserve to act as a ballast. We want the maximum drawdown of the account to be 20 percent. The account is a combination of the portion exposed to risk in trades that produce drawdown and the amount held risk-free with no drawdown. The higher safe-f, the lower the drawdowns in trades. Setting a lower limit of 0.66 on safe-f restricts to those series with drawdowns in the trade portion of the equity curve less than 30 percent (20% / 0.66 = 30%).

- Liquidity and bid-ask spread. For the examples here, the limit was set at $5,000,000 per day, on average for the most recent three months. Choose limits appropriate for your trading.

Setting control variables for accuracy to 65% and holding period to 5 days, none of the roughly 5000 issues we tested passed the screens.

Resetting accuracy to 75% and holding period to 5 days, several hundred passed.

There are two reasons issues failed to pass the screen.

One is inadequate profit potential. The CAR25 is below the level that can provide a return that exceeds a risk-free alternative without exceeding the stated risk tolerance. These issues can be ignored—they will not be profitable using any model.

The second is history shorter than eight years. There are issues that pass the CAR25 screen but fail the 2000 day screen. Some of these are good candidates for trading, and you might want to use them. If you do, be rigorous in validating the system. Since most of their history is in a period when the broad market moved strongly in one direction, there is a greater chance a system trading them will fail in other market conditions.

Figure 2.28 lists a 50 issue subset that have the highest safe-f, highest CAR25, and seem to be relatively easy to model.

ADP	EWJ	K	RE	VPU
ATO	EWM	KMB	SJM	VTV
AZN	EWS	LG	SWX	VUG
AZO	GAS	MDY	SXT	VZ
BDX	GPC	MGLN	THI	WABC
BTI	HCN	NU	UPS	WGL
CEF	IVV	OEF	VDC	XLI
DEO	IWB	PEP	VGT	XLP
EE	IXJ	PJP	VHT	XLU
EWH	IYH	PTP	VIG	XLV

Figure 2.28 List of issues that are good candidates for development

Which Issues are "Best?"

We do not know yet, but we are narrowing the field. What we do know is that the issues that passed the screens and are listed in Figure 2.28 are best in terms of the first two goldilocks characteristics. They have high profit potential without excessive volatility.

To be profitable as components of a trading system, there must be identifiable patterns that precede the price changes. It is the model that has the logic and rules that identify patterns and generate buy and sell signals. We will not know how much of the potential can be captured until the data series is combined with a model to form a trading system.

Holding Longer

There are many reasons for holding positions longer than a few days. There may be restrictions that forbid or penalties that discourage selling a position earlier than some limit. You may have read or heard an anecdote where a large profit was made as a result of holding a position for a long time.

Large profits improve any trading system. But limiting losses is more critical than achieving gains. As holding periods increase, adverse price movements increase in proportion to the square root of the holding period, just from the random changes in prices. If a series of trades that hold 5 days has intra-trade drawdowns of, say, 4 percent, we can expect that a series of trades over the same data where the trades are held 20 days will have intra-trade drawdowns of 8 percent. If an error is made predicting whether a trade will be a winner or a loser, losers that are held 20 days will have losses double those of losers held 5 days.

The math is pretty clear—the sweet spot in terms of maximum profit for a specified level of risk is a holding period of few days. And until the holding period is very short, where transactional costs erode profits, shorter is better.

Nevertheless, you may ask, what are the implications of insisting on a longer holding period? Say one calendar month—21 trading days.

The CAR is limited by position size, which is limited by risk, which is limited by the inherent characteristics of a price series for a given trade accuracy and holding period. So far, we have been estimating CAR for a fixed risk tolerance. We can use the same simulation to test other settings. If the holding period must be 21 trading days, we can fix that variable and examine CAR versus risk.

Given a set of trades, or well defined potential trades, and a risk tolerance, safe-f is completely determined. Safe-f is the highest fractional position size that places the CDF of drawdown no higher than the 5% / 20% point defined by the risk tolerance statement.

Given a set of trades, or well defined potential trades, and a value of safe-f, the CDF of profit is completely determined. CAR25 is completely determined.

For SPY, using a risk tolerance of 5% / 20% / 2 years, 70% accuracy, 21 day holding period, based on 1/1/1999 through 1/1/2012, the safe-f fraction is 0.563 and CAR25 is 5.4%. The CDF of drawdown is shown in Figure 2.29.

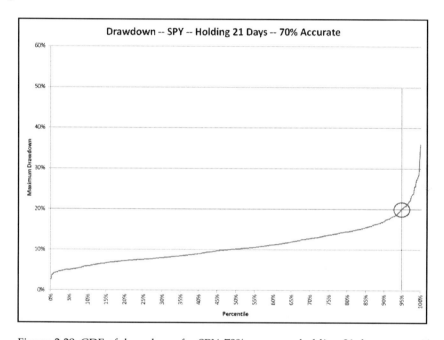

Figure 2.29 CDF of drawdown for SPY, 70% accuracy, holding 21 days

No other assumptions are necessary to produce the CDF of profit. It is shown in Figure 2.30. We can read CAR25 from the curve. It is 5.4%

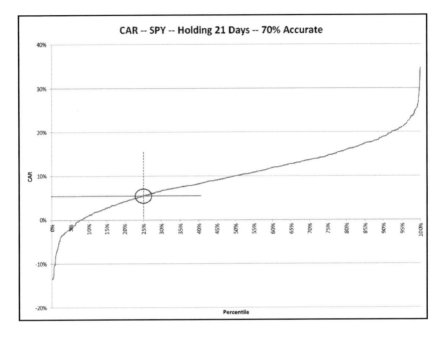

Figure 2.30 CDF of Compound Annual Rate of Return, 70%, 21 days

If we want to change the value of CAR25 without changing the trades, we must change the position size fraction. There is no other knob to turn. For a given set of trades, position size completely determines the position of the CDF. To increase CAR25 is to drag the entire CDF of profit upward, as illustrated in Figure 2.31. Fraction is increased from 0.563 to 1.000—take all trades with all available funds.

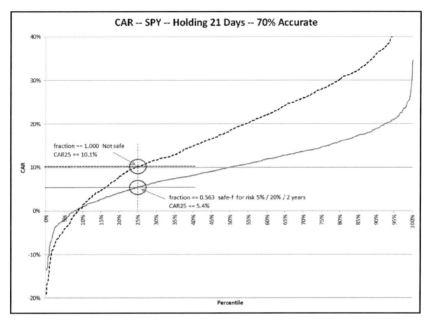

Figure 2.31 CDF of CAR, fraction increased to 1.000

Changing the fraction changes the position of the CDF of risk. Those two curves are linked together. Intended or not, changing one changes the other, as shown in Figure 2.32.

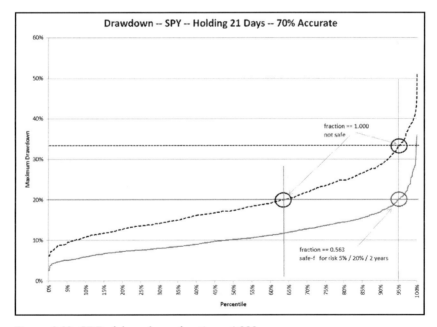

Figure 2.32 CDF of drawdown fraction = 1.000

Traded at full fraction, position size is no longer safe. Risk of drawdown at the 5% level (95th percentile) has increased from 20% to 34%. Seen another way, risk of 20% drawdown has increased from 5% to 37% (95th to 63rd percentile). These are represented by the two circles on the dotted line.

Potential CAR at full fraction is 10.1%, before application of a yet-to-be-developed model. Increasing CAR further requires either increasing position size above 1.00—by using margin, trading an ETF with a beta greater than 1, or using options—or increasing accuracy of trades selected beyond 70%.

Accuracy at 90% increases CAR25 to 21.8 at safe-f with a fraction of 0.779. Accuracy at 95% increases CAR25 to 35.5 at safe-f of 1.000.

The task of predicting whether the price of SPY will be higher or lower one month ahead with 70 percent accuracy, or higher, is daunting. It has left the realm of technical analysis. I know of no indicators that accurate that far in the future.

We might have expected that all we needed to do was increase our tolerance limit and we would see profit potential rise. At ordinary levels of accuracy, that is not what we found. Accuracy of 60% holding 21 days did not show profit potential at any level of risk. Profit potential at 70% accuracy is marginal. Profit potential begins to rise in step with willingness to accept additional risk at 80% accuracy, and even those values are not worth the risk. Increasing risk tolerance for a poor system does not increase profit—it only increases risk and drawdown.

My conclusion is that holding through 21 days is too difficult, or too risky, or insufficiently profitable. 21 days is too long a holding period.

In my opinion, and supported by the math, it appears that holding positions in SPY for 21 days with reasonable risk and CAR greater than risk-free bank interest is not achievable. No matter how much we wish it would be.

Chapter 3 — Trading System Development

The trading system development procedure is an extensive in-sample data mining and (hopefully) learning process:

- Generate many alternative trading systems (ATS), each based on a specific model-data combiination.
- Evaluate each ATS, giving each a score computed by the objective function.
- Rank the ATSs, preferring those with high scores, selecting one.

Followed by limited (ideally one time only) testing of the selected system using out-of-sample data to validate that the system has learned.

Figure 3.1 shows the flowchart of trading system development.

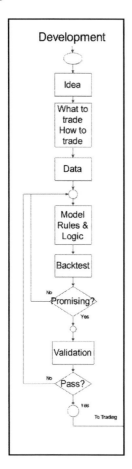

Figure 3.1 Flowchart of Trading System Development

The Model

Central to the development is the model. The model's purpose is to identify patterns that precede profitable trades. First to learn to identify those patterns using historical data. Then to recognize those same patterns in real-time data.

Input to the model is price and volume data representing trades. Output is a series of signals telling the trader when to be long, flat, and short. Internally, the model is a set of mathematical relationships that transform input to output—price and volume to signals, then to trades.

The model typically includes formulas that manipulate the raw data, consolidating and aligning it as necessary, transforming it and creating indicators from it to increase its ability to detect patterns. Patterns are filtered through a set of rules to generate the signals, then reported as trades. The scientific method of data-driven adjustment and validation is clearly present.

Models come in many varieties. Traditional development platforms have a limited number of *model paradigms* built in to them. The most common is *decision tree*, where a tree-like structure of comparisons and questions leads to a specific value of the signal for that data bar. Machine learning adds other model paradigms that can be chosen and used, such as *linear regression*, *neural network*, and *support vector machines*.

All models are, or at least can be expressed as, a set of mathematical operations. Generation of signals is essentially a linear algebra task involving solution of a set of simultaneous equations.

Models and the Premises

The underlying assumptions of technical analysis were listed in Chapter 1. Some commentary and a diagram might help understanding how the assumptions fit into the development process. Going point by point with each assumption, then explanation:

☆ The markets we model are sufficiently inefficient for us to make a profit trading them.

   Our success in profitable trading will tell us our answer. If we are able to develop a profitable trading system, that is evidence that the market is not efficient.

☆ There is information—*patterns*—in the historical price series that can be used to identify profitable trading opportunities.

   There are two parts to this—profitable trades and patterns. Begin with profitable trades.

   Figure 3.2 shows the daily close of SPY for a period of six months. Assume we plan to trade SPY, taking a long position at the close of those days when tomorrow's close will be higher than today's close. The periods of rising closing prices are the profitable trades we want the model to identify. They are marked with the larger circles.

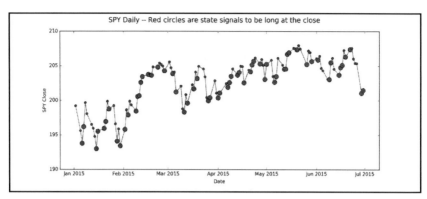

Figure 3.2 Desirable trades

If patterns that precede those trades do exist, the model must find them.

☆ Trading systems can be designed to recognize the patterns and give buy and sell signals.

The patterns might be found in or derived from the price data series, or they might come from the other auxiliary data series.

This is the "data in", "recognize pattern", "signal out" part of the system. Some reasons why it is not easy are:

❒ The data being used might not contain an identifiable pattern that precedes the trades you want to identify.

❒ The data is noisy. We are searching for a weak signal in a noisy background. See the section "The Signal and the Noise" in Chapter 1.

❒ The data might change characteristics over the period we are searching. See the section "Stationarity" in Chapter 1.

❒ The data is ambiguous. Given a particular pattern, say the crossing of an RSI indicator with a given level, in some cases the next day the price is rising, and in others the next day it is falling. See the section "Indicators" below.

❒ The model might overfit the in-sample data used during development, memorizing the data but failing to learn, then be unable to identify profitable patterns in out-of-sample data.

❒ The model might need modification. It might need to be simpler, more complex, or use a different learning technique.

☆ Patterns similar to those found in the historical data will continue to be found in future data.

No matter how accurately the model detects the signals that precede profitable trades during development, we cannot make profitable trades unless the future resembles the past. See the section "Stationarity" in Chapter 1.

What I Would Like to Know

A model is based on an idea. When I am leaving on a trip, I know the destination, and I have an estimate of the route, travel time, etc, before leaving the driveway. Similarly, my trading model begins with an idea and I use that to guide me.

Not all ideas are achievable. I might want a system where I can buy one stock or fund, hold it long enough to qualify for favorable tax benefits, minimize attention to the holding, have a high return, and have low drawdown. Much as I might want that, it is not achievable.

A more practical approach is to ask myself a question, the answer to which would help develop an achievable system, then answer the question and build the model accordingly.

For example.

Q. What would I like to know about tomorrow? What would I do if I knew?

A. I would like to know whether tomorrow's closing price for the issue, yet to be selected, will be higher than today's closing price.

If I knew, I would trade at the close of the trading day. I would use daily data available at the close of trading, taking a long position when the signal indicated a rise, remaining flat when it did not. I would reevaluate each day, holding long when I received successive positive signals, going flat upon receiving the first non-positive signal.

My system development would be guided in an attempt to gather information needed to answer the question.

Unfortunately, some combinations of risk, reward, and trading style we might want are just not possible. The risk assessment will let us know.

Traditional Development Platforms

Until a few years ago, trading system models were developed nearly exclusively using development platforms—special purpose computer programs specifically created for trading. These platforms have features and functions built into them to handle data, display charts, compute indicators, build mathematical relationships, generate signals, create trades, and report performance.
• The model is decision tree.

- The paradigm is "compute an indicator, then see what follows."
- The signals they produce are impulses that identify categories—buy, sell, short, cover. See the section "Impulse and State Signals," below.

Much of the early literature describing these models assumed:
- The patterns were fairly well defined and stood out from the noise.
- Successful indicators had long lookback periods and changed slowly.
- Holding periods for trades were relatively long.

Additionally, many analysts made unrealistic assumptions:
- Traditional wisdom does not require validation.
- A small number of anecdotal examples provide valuable forecasting.
- Relationships were, and would continue to be, stationary.
- Systems that worked once will continue to work indefinitely.
- Systems will always recover from drawdowns.
- Drawdowns are opportunities to increase position size and recover lost funds.

Figure 3.3, a repeat of Figure 1.4, is a schematic showing a trading system model of the type associated with traditional trading system development platforms. Examples of this type of platform are AmiBroker, NinjaTrader, and TradeStation.

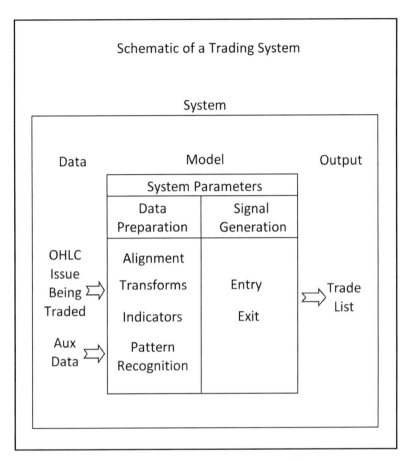

Figure 3.3 Schematic Showing a Trading System Model

Machine Learning Platforms

As markets are becoming more efficient, patterns are becoming harder to distinguish. Trading is more frequent, and holding periods shorter. Machine learning techniques are being adapted to trading. Machine learning gives new ways to identify profitable patterns. Ways that are more accurate and less prone to overfitting.

These are still the early days in machine learning platforms that include tools specific to trading. Data handling, charting, and functions related to analysis of trades are still somewhat rudimentary and the platforms lack the full set of features trading system developers want. These limitations are compensated for by the broad variety of models available, and the ability to perform multiple phase simulations in the same program run as pattern recognition.

- The model is supervised learning using any of the twenty or more machine learning techniques, including decision trees, neural networks, support vector machines, and random forests.
- The mathematical relationships are systems of simultaneous equations.
- The paradigm is "identify desirable trades, then see what happened earlier."
- The signals are categories representing states—beLong, beFlat, beShort.

Interchangeability

Figure 3.4 shows how the two—indicator-based development using traditional platforms and machine learning development—relate to each other and fit into model development. Techniques used for issue selection and data preparation are the same. At the conclusion of validation, both produce a best estimate set of trades. The similarity should not be surprising, since decision tree is one of the machine learning techniques.

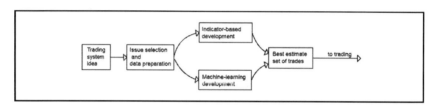

Figure 3.4 Two paths for model development

The choice of which development platform to use is yours. Whether you decide to use a traditional trading system development platform or machine learning, use the scientific method. Figure 3.5 is a repeat of Figure 1.1.

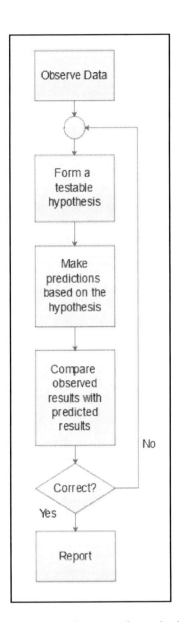

Figure 3.5 The scientific method

Impulse and State Signals

The system represented by the schematic in Figure 3.3 above uses *impulse* signals to identify entry into and exit from a trade. The alternative is *state* signals.

Impulse signals identify transitions, such as the beginning or end of a trade. They arise from an event that occurs on a single bar—such as when an RSI indicator falls through a critical level. An impulse signal occurs once on the bar when the rules of the model are satisfied—one impulse for the entry, and one impulse for the exit. In general, there are no additional signals between the entry and the exit. (Although there could be additional entry signals.) Impulse signals are associated with actions—buy, sell, short, and cover.

Impulse signals define trades. In evaluation of the system's trades, a data point is a *trade*—however many days that trade lasts.

State signals are also defined by the rules of the model. While impulse signals identify boundaries, state signals identify conditions—such as whether the position to be held for the next day is long, flat, or short. There is a state signal for every day.

Given the same indicators and patterns, trades signalled by state signals and marking to market daily hold positions for the same period as trades signalled by impulse signals. In the evaluation of the system's trades when using state signals, a data point is a *day*—however many days that trade lasts.

The two are equivalent for many purposes. We can easily convert from impulse to state by changing state at the first occurrence of an impulse, then holding that same state until the first occurrence of an impulse that changes to a new position.

Your trading system development platform probably has functions that allow you to create state or impulse signals, as you wish, and to convert between them.

The bar-by-bar account equity is identical whether a trade is denoted by impulse or state signals. Refer to the section "Mark-to-Market Equivalence" in Chapter 2.

Figure 3.6 illustrates a multi-day trade with corresponding state and impulse signals.

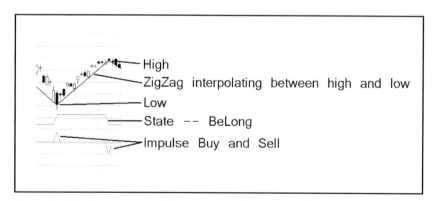

Figure 3.6 Multi-day trade with impulse and state signals

Changing from impulse signals to state signals changes the way we view trades—from some number of bars between the buy and sell impulses, where there is no action and no opportunity for trade management, to a series of single-day marked-to-market trades.

When a sequence of days has the same state, the position is held over and appears as a single multi-day trade. With state signals, there will be as many trade-related data points as days the system holds an open position.

Using state signals, every day is evaluated on its own. With the exception of trades that are open across the boundaries of the test period, performance results are identical.

There are significant advantages to using state signals over impulse signals.

- A state signal is generated for each and every bar, giving the trader a clear indication of the correct position for the next bar, and coordinating measurement of the system with management of the system.

- During testing, a period of time is defined and trades that occur within that period are evaluated. Only those trades that are completely within the test period can be correctly and accurately evaluated.

    The edges of the test period create distortions. Because indicators, parameters, and rules often change as a new test period is entered, the platform cannot determine that a trade was open in the previous period and should be continued. The first trade of each period begins with the first new signal of the period. Similarly, a trade that is open at the end of a test period can either be artificially closed or completely ignored.

    When impulse signals are used, periods where a trade was held at either end of a test period are not accurately evaluated.

    When state signals are used, there is at most one day lost at each end of the test period.

- Impulse signals work well with traditional development platforms because the platforms were developed with the expectation that trades would identify buy and sell points. State signals work equally well with traditional platforms.

- State signals are particularly well suited for use with machine learning platforms where it is important to have a target value for each bar to guide the learning.

- An advantage to state signals is increased opportunity for control of trade management throughout the trade. The health of the system is reevaluated every day at the same time it is marked-to-market. This is also the frequency that position size is readjusted using the dynamic position sizing technique used to calculate safe-f for the next trade.

Learning

Learning is the process of examining data, recognizing some patterns, observing related patterns, resulting in *generalization*—the ability to recognize patterns in data not previously seen. As it applies to trading systems, we will be looking for patterns that provide either:

- *Classification.* Buy or Sell. Either to open a new position or to close an existing position. The issue of how much to buy or sell—position sizing—is addressed separately from pattern recognition.
- *Estimation.* Direction and magnitude of change anticipated. If an estimation technique is used in the trading system, we may apply a threshold filter to convert the estimation into a classification category. Estimation is used in the trading management system to specify the position size for the next trade.

Learning is not possible unless there is data to be examined and patterns to find. Preferably a lot of data and a lot of examples. This is definitely a data mining activity. The data mined is called the *in-sample* data. We are searching for patterns within the historical price data that precede profitable trades.

We cannot learn a feature that has not been seen. The in-sample data must include examples of the patterns to be learned.

Identifying patterns in the in-sample data is necessary for learning, but is not sufficient. There must be generalization. The test for generalization is validation. That is, testing previously unused data to estimate the success of detecting the patterns and defining the rules. The data tested for validation is called the *out-of-sample* data.

Validation is the step designed to provide the confidence requested in the goal.

Objective Function

Objective functions are extremely important both in trading system development and later in trading management. There are many millions of combinations of data series, rules, and parameters, each one of which defines a trading system. Which is best?

The trading system development process consists of generating many ATSs—combinations of data series, indicators, rules, and parameters—and choosing the best from among them.

Best, seen from trading results, is subjective. It includes positive growth of the trading account, limited drawdowns to the trading account, and conformity of results to real or artificially imposed constraints such as trading frequency and holding period.

Best, seen from within the development process, is the score computed using an objective function and associated with each of the alternatives being compared.

Compared with many decisions we must make in life, trading system development is relatively easy. The common unit of measurement is dollars, or your currency equivalent. Winning trades gain dollars, losing trades cost dollars. Personal risk tolerance sets a lower threshold. Provided that risk threshold is not violated in the time period, higher gains are better, the highest gain is the best.

CAR25 is the risk-normalized estimate of profit potential that I prefer as my objective function. See the section "CAR25—Universal Objective Function," in Chapter 1.

If you are using machine learning and working in a language such as Python, you probably have access to everything required to compute CAR25.

If you cannot compute CAR25 for some reason, but you can define and compute a custom objective function, reward those characteristics of trades you prefer, penalize or omit those you do not prefer. In particular, avoid rewarding alternatives whose scores are high because of the specific sequence of trades discovered in the test.

If you cannot define a custom objective function, use the best available from those provided by the development platform.

There might be limitations. Trading system development platforms vary in their capability to define, calculate, and reference custom objective functions during development test runs. Objective functions provided with the platform usually include net profit or final equity. Run some tests early in the development to see whether these objective functions work well. Net profit and final equity, among others, reward alternatives that are overfit to the in-sample data and perform poorly out-of-sample.

When working with a traditional trading system development platform (at least those available today), direct calculation of CAR25 is not possible. The objective function that is used for automated searching and evaluation during backtesting and optimization runs must be defined from those metrics provided by the platform.

Some platforms, such as AmiBroker, provide easy access to a rich selection of metrics, allow custom objective functions that include those metrics, and then use your custom objective function to guide optimization. This is one of the very important capabilities a trading system development platform should have. It is one of the reasons I prefer and recommend AmiBroker.

Assuming you are working with a trading system development platform that provides a rich variety of metrics, what makes a good objective function?

The model identifies patterns, issues buy and sell signals, resulting in a sequence of trades. Even if you cannot compute CAR25 directly, you can choose characteristics that give high CAR25 scores. They are:
- We know that relying on the single specific sequence of trades is misleading, so do not use metrics that are sequence dependent. That excludes maximum series drawdown. But it does not exclude trade-by-trade loss or maximum adverse excursion.
- Reward gain and penalize loss. Do not penalize gain. Exclude Sharpe ratio, but not necessarily Sortino ratio.
- TWR = G ^ N. G should be high, after transactional costs. Insist on a positive expectation. N should be high, so trade frequently.
- Drawdown increases in proportion to the square root of holding period. Reward short holding periods.
- It is psychologically easier to trade a system with a high percentage of winning trades. Reward a high ratio of winning trades.
- Determination of system health is easier when accuracy is high. Reward a high ratio of winning trades.
- The sweet spot for risk inherent in a data series is high accuracy and short holding period.
- Avoiding *toxic trades*—large losing trades—is important. Penalize large losses.

The list of features to be rewarded includes:
- Trade frequently.
- Trade accurately.
- Hold a short period.
- Have a high gain per trade.

The list of features to be penalized centers on losing trades:
- Maximum trade drawdown or maximum adverse excursion.
- Average loss of losing trades.
- Worst loss.

Look for metrics provided by your platform that allow you to identify and weight these features.

The Population and the Sample

The price series itself defines the profit that can potentially be captured by a trading system. The analysis by the prospector in Chapter 2 gave some estimate of what is possible. Figure 3.7 shows a cloud of large and small plus and minus characters. They are the *population* of price changes for that issue. For the given time period, these represent the price changes in a data series. They are there whether we trade them or not.

The data is divided into in-sample and out-of-sample areas. During model development, the area to the left of the wavy line is used to build alternative systems.

Some of the characters have an "s" character with them. The "s" represents the price changes that were signaled to be long positions by the trading system. As you would expect, it got some right and some wrong.

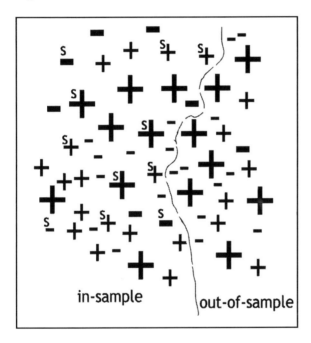

Figure 3.7 Price changes signalled by a trading system

Those price changes marked with "s" become the trades resulting from the model applied to that data series. That set of trades is the *sample*. One of the goals of modeling is to learn characteristics of the population by studying the sample.

The signals are defined by the trading system. Every signal is attached to a price change and becomes a trade. If the system is accurate, the model identifies patterns predominantly associated with profitable price changes.

As the creation and testing of alternative models in carried out, each alternative produces a different set of signals resulting in a different set of trades. A different portion of the in-sample population is marked with "s." Each set of trades defines a distribution—a sample of price changes drawn from a distribution of the population of price changes.

Because we create and test—in-sample testing and data mining—so many alternative trading systems, we eventually discover some that have high objective function scores. Those signals fit those price changes very well. If we examined all possible samples, we would see that the ones we liked best came from the optimistic tail. In-sample results are always good. We do not stop fooling with the system until they are good.

Parameters

You are already familiar with parameters that control functions and indicators. The length of a moving average or the lookback period for an RSI indicator, for example. These are determined through parameter selection, backtesting, and optimization as part of trading system development. The process, discussed further below, is:
*   Set limits for a range of values.
*   Search through those values.
*   Create an alternative model for each.
*   Compute an objective function score for each.
*   Rank according to the objective function score.
*   Choose the highest ranked alternative as the preferred system.

Choosing Hyperparameters

There are choices made even earlier in the development process that have great influence on the system and its profitability. These involve higher level aspects of the system and are not easily included in the optimization phase. Examples include choices of the length of the in-sample and out-of-sample periods, and the model paradigm to use. These are called *hyperparameters*. The technique used to decide which of these alternatives to use is *crossvalidation*.

The crossvalidation process is done in two phases. An outer phase controls the hyperparameter being determined and runs a loop, one inner phase run for each value of the alternative hyperparameter values being considered.

The inner phase divides the data into a number of *folds* or partitions. An iterative process makes as many passes over the data as there are folds. For each pass:
*   Set one of the folds aside to be used for out-of-sample evaluation.
*   Using the remaining folds, train the model.
*   Using the trained model, evaluate the fold that was set aside.

When all folds have been evaluated, compute the metric for that value of the hyperparameter.

I recommend reading the slide presentations of Dr. Ricardo Gutierrez-Osuna[1] and Dr. Andrew Moore[2]. The material on the scikit-learn site also has a good description of the process[3].

Crossvalidation is regularly used in machine learning model development.

It is seldom used in traditional trading system development, for one of several reasons:
- The need for it has not been recognized.
- Designing the trading system platform itself to include crossvalidation capabilities adds to the complexity of the platform.
- Some of the choices have been made by the publisher of the platform and hard coded into it. In a completely open development environment, the choice of which model paradigm to use would be determined through a series of tests, compared using crossvalidation. In traditional trading system development platforms, the only model implemented is decision tree, so you have no choices to make of which model to use.

The most important hyperparameter for a traditional platform is length of period of stationarity. Unfortunately, stationarity has been largely ignored by analysts developing trading systems using traditional platforms. But, as explained earlier, for a trading system to be profitable in live trading, the distribution of signals must be stationary over the combined length of the in-sample and out-of-sample period. While a model can be fit to any set of data, the profitability of the resulting system depends very much on how closely the future resembles the past. Not addressing stationarity results in an assumption that the distributions being analyzed are stationary. If, however, they are not stationary, the system will not be profitable.

If you are using machine learning, your development program can include crossvalidation to choose these hyperparameters:
- The model paradigm.
- The length of time the signal is stationary.

If you are using a traditional trading system development platform, your choices of model will be limited to those built-in—decision tree

---

1   Gutierrez-Osuna, Ricardo, Texas A&M University, *Lecture 13: Validation*.

2   Moore, Andrew, Carnegie Mellon University, *Cross-validation for detecting and preventing overfitting*.

3   http://scikit-learn.org/stable/modules/cross_validation.html

for certain, and perhaps one or two others. Test those individually. Determination of the length of stationarity will require separate programming and test runs outside the development platform.

For additional discussion of stationarity, watch my YouTube video[4].

In-sample Data Length

The signal or pattern component of the data must be stationary throughout the in-sample training period. The in-sample period may be shorter than the period of synchronization, but avoid longer periods. The issue is not the length of the period in days so much as it is the length of the period of stationarity.

Naive developers are sometimes heard to recommend using as much data and as long a period as possible for each test period. Their reasoning is that the model will be exposed to as many different conditions as possible and will be able to perform well in all of them. That is the wrong view. A period with multiple conditions is the definition of non-stationarity. Using data that includes many different conditions decreases the fit to any of the conditions. In a phrase, ambiguous, conflicting, inconsistent, or stale data is worse than no data. Test periods—particularly in-sample periods over which the model is fit to the data—should be as short as practical. The best models use short periods and regularly resynchronize the rules and parameters to keep the model tuned to the signal.

Out-of-sample Data Length

Unfortunately, out-of-sample performance is usually poor. That is, of all the alternative models we apply to a series of data during in-sample data mining, most do not identify patterns that precede profitable trades out-of-sample. Either they are fit to noise—to non-recurring patterns unique to the specific data being tested—or the characteristics of the data have changed by the end of the period and the profitable patterns do not persist beyond it.

To be useful for trading, the signals must exist in the data and be identifiable beyond the in-sample period, and those signals must be profitable.

There are no rules, or even rules-of-thumb, for estimating the length of time a model will continue to be profitable out-of-sample. Only monitoring the performance of the system over time gives us that information.

In any event, that length is non-stationary and changes as characteristics of the data change. If the system falls out of synchronization before the end of the out-of-sample period, the day-to-day monitoring

4   Bandy, Howard, *The Importance of Being Stationary*, YouTube Video, 2015.

of system health and associated risk will cause safe-f to drop and the system will be taken offline. This is part of the dynamic position sizing technique.

There is no minimum length for the out-of-sample period. It is, or at least can be, appropriate to treat each day as a one-day long out-of-sample period, with parameter values readjusted daily.

In general, the lengths of the in-sample and out-of-sample periods are related only to the extent that the system must remain stationary and synchronized for the total length of those two periods.

Longer Holding Periods

One thing you can expect is that longer holding periods require longer periods of stationarity. That implies both longer in-sample periods, and longer out-of-sample periods. Increasing the length of time increases the probability that conditions change, stationarity is lost, and profitability drops. Also, drawdown increases as holding period increases. Longer holding periods imply greater risk, smaller safe-f, and lower CAR25.

Number of Data Points

Again, we have a familiar tradeoff. We want more data points for finer granularity, better precision, and easier statistical significance. But not so many data points that some of them represent conditions that are no longer current.

There must be data points in every test period. At least several, preferably many.

If you are using impulse signals, trading frequency and holding period affect test period length. Each data point is a trade that is both opened and closed within the test period.

The longer positions are held:
- The longer the test period must be to span several trades.
- The greater the intra-trade drawdown.

The longer the test period, the more likely the model and the data will lose synchronization.

A system that trades a single issue long / flat, trades frequently, and holds a few days, might complete 15 to 20 trades in each year. In-sample length might be one year—perhaps as short as a few months. Out-of-sample length a few months or longer.

Contrast with a system that holds several months. The in-sample length must be several years, and the out-of-sample period long enough to include several trades.

If you are using state signals, each data point is a mark-to-market period. You have much more flexibility in setting the length of both the in-sample and out-of-sample periods, even for trades that are held for a long time.

Indicators

Indicators can be based on anything—price, volume, patterns, calendar, multiple time frames, auxiliary data, diffusion indexes. Indicators are most useful when they have significant events, such as crossings or bottoms, at about the same frequency as the trades we hope to identify.

Filters are similar to indicators in most aspects, but change state less frequently.

Ideal Indicator

Assume we want to predict extreme oversold, enter at the close of a day when the price is at a near-bottom in anticipation of a price rise, and exit the next day. We are looking ahead one day at a time.

Entry is based on an indicator that oscillates with about the same frequency as the trades we are looking for. At this level of activity, all indicators based on price (z-score, RSI, stochastic, %B, detrended oscillator, etc.) are interchangeable. Pick one to work with. Techniques that relax the requirement that lookback periods for indicators be integers, such as the CustomRSI described in my Mean Reversion book[5], allow greater flexibility in tuning indicators to data. For this example, we will use the very popular 2-period RSI.

Ideally, there would be a clear relationship between the value of an indicator, such as the RSI2, and the price change the day ahead. Figure 3.8 shows how it would look, where:

GainAhead = 100 * (Ref(C,1)-C) / C

C is today's closing price. Ref(C,1) is the close 1 day in the future.

---

5   Bandy, Howard, *Mean Reversion Trading Systems*, Blue Owl Press, 2013.

In a perfect world, there is a perfect relationship between the ideal indicator and the gain for the day ahead. The indicator-day ahead data
points are the dots that form the straight line.

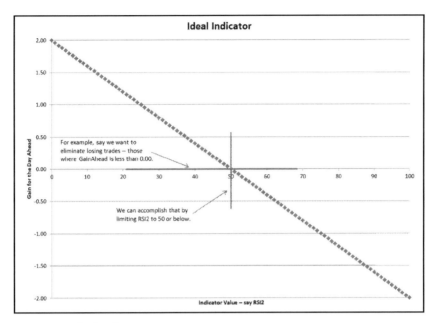

Figure 3.8 Ideal indicator

We want to take all winning trades (those above the horizontal line)
and eliminate all losing trades (those below the horizontal line). We
can accomplish that by taking long positions only when RSI2 is below
50, those trades to the left of the vertical line.

Fuzzy Indicator

With just a little fuzziness in the data, as shown in Figure 3.9, the indicator is less accurate. The indicator-day ahead data points are again the dots, but they are no longer a perfectly straight line.

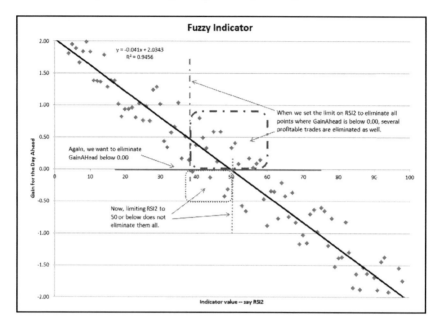

Figure 3.9 Slightly fuzzy indicator

The solid diagonal line shows the linear regression fit to the data points. The r-squared statistic is 0.94—a very good fit by most standards. Again, we want to eliminate losing trades using the same indicator. When we set RSI2 to 50, the dotted vertical line, the result is not perfect. Not all of the losing trades are eliminated, and some winning trades are eliminated. When the limit on RSI2 is changed so that it does eliminate all of the losing trades, the dashed vertical line at about 39, a side effect is that a large number of winning trades—those in the large dashed area—are also eliminated.

Realistic Indicator

Figure 3.10 shows the relationship between GainAhead and the RSI2 indicator for the actual data for SPY for several years. When a trading system rule states we should hold a long position whenever RSI2 is less than 36, this is the data it is using.

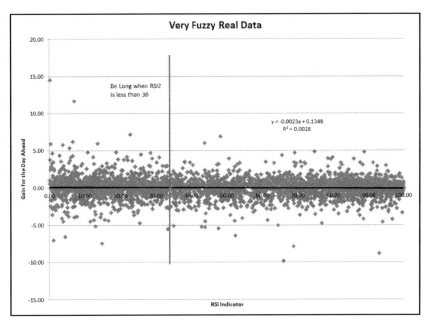

Figure 3.10 Very fuzzy real data

The trendline shows an r-squared of 0.0028. This is essentially zero and was in the round-off error of the 0.94 value shown in Figure 3.9. The vertical line is set at 36, the value determined during system development.

Looking at Figure 3.10, there is no apparent best place to set the vertical line that limits RSI2. The relationship is a little clearer when the 1146 pairs of RSI2 and GainAhead are sorted by RSI2 and combined into bins of 5 RSI units. As Figure 3.11 shows, there is a net positive gain of about 136 "gain ahead points" from being long when RSI2 is less than 36.

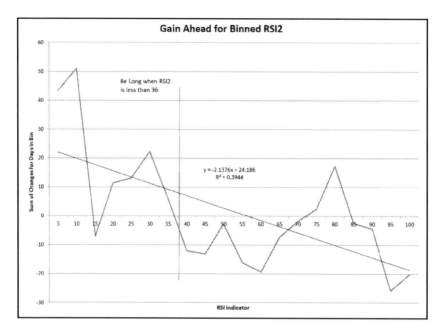

Figure 3.11 Gain ahead for binned RSI2

This illustrates several points:

- Based on traditional frequentist statistical analysis, waiting until the end of the data period, and treating the relationship as stationary, the correlation between RSI2 and GainAhead is indistinguishable from random.
- Even for a relationship between indicator and profit that is known to be tradable, there is remarkably little "edge."
- Anything we can do to improve the relationship will be immensely profitable.

Transformations

A transformation is a mathematical operation—a functional relationship. For a given set or distribution of input values, a transformation applies a formula to each input value to compute a set or distribution of corresponding output values.

The reason for using transformations is to make the data a better predictor. Transforming an indicator changes the shape of the pdf or, equivalently, the CDF. The transformed distribution has a higher or lower percentage of values in some areas, typically at the extremes, than the original indicator.

There are an infinite number of transformations. Think of transforming an indicator, or any data series, as measuring that indicator using a different scale on the ruler; or as focusing a camera before taking the picture. John Tukey, an American mathematician who made many contributions to data analysis in the late 20th century, called them re-expressions. A common everyday transformation is converting temperature from degrees Fahrenheit to degrees Celsius. Examples in our context:

- Input might be price and output the RSI(price). Indicators are themselves transformations.
- Input might be the RSI value, output the rank of the RSI value. The transformation changes the distribution of the indicator to make the signals clearer.
- Input might be OHLC price bars, output a metric of trade profit and risk. The transformation creates a new target to better judge trade quality.

Note that every transformation introduces some bias and distortion. This is intentional. Our goal is practical, not theoretical. The measure of our success is in the performance of the resulting trading system.

Out-of-range Values

The input set is a sample—a subset of a population or universe. In some cases we are certain what the minimum and maximum values of additional data, such as that in out-of-sample periods, will be. RSI, for example, is always between 0 and 100. In other cases, we cannot be certain. Values of %B, for example, are concentrated between 0 and 100, but can be less than 0 or greater than 100. Some trading system indicators, transformations, and rules require the data they process have values guaranteed to be within a defined range. The transformation of range must be able to assign a consistent, accurate, deterministic output value corresponding to any input value, even those outside the expected range. Figure 3.12 shows where this is important.

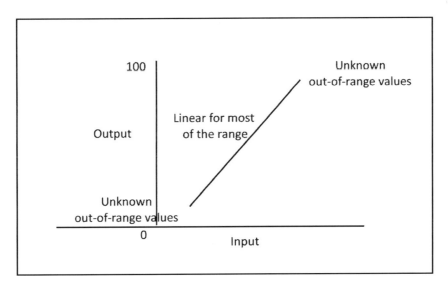

Figure 3.12 -- Anticipating Out-of-Range Values

There are three alternative methods to do this.

Omit or Ignore

All of the price data used in a trading system has already been aligned to a common series, such as SPY, to ensure there is a data bar and a price for every period of trading. As indicators are being computed, every bar must have an indicator value that can be interpreted reasonably, even if it is a default value or a copy of the value from the previous bar. Ignoring or omitting effectively removes that bar, which is not a reasonable option.

Clip or Winsorize

Winsorizing is the process of replacing every value that is too low and out of range by the lower limit defined for the output range, and replacing every value that is too high and out of range by the upper limit defined by the output range.   All of the left tail data points are given the same low value; and all of the right tail data points are given the same high value. There are drawbacks to Winsorizing that make it a poor choice for our application:

- It fails to preserve the order of the transformed data.

- It fails to distinguish between data points at the extremes—precisely where overbought and oversold are most likely to be identified.

Squash—the Logistic Function

This transformation maintains as much of the linear relationship (the long straight portion of the transfer function before it begins curving) as possible, while accommodating unknown out-of-range values, however extreme they may be.

While it might be possible to create a function that mated long, tapered sections on the right and left with the linear section in the center, a better solution is to use the *logistic function*.

The logistic function is one of a class of functions called *sigmoid*. Individual sigmoid functions vary in the output range (some are -1 to +1, others 0 to 1), in the steepness of the transition from lower to upper extreme, and in the portion that is linear.

The formula for the version of the logistic function used in this example is:

$$y(x) = \frac{1}{1 + e^{-x}}$$

The input data in the example shown in Figure 3.13 ranges from -10 to +10 (the horizontal axis), but in practice there is no upper or lower limit. The logistic function transforms whatever input data is passed to it, giving output between 0.0 and 1.0. That value is multiplied by 100 before plotting (vertical axis). Note how the values near the center of the input range, which is near zero, are given a linear transformation, while extreme input values are squashed into the output range, but order is preserved.

Figure 3.13 shows the plot of the logistic function. The length of the section that is linear is about six standard deviations.

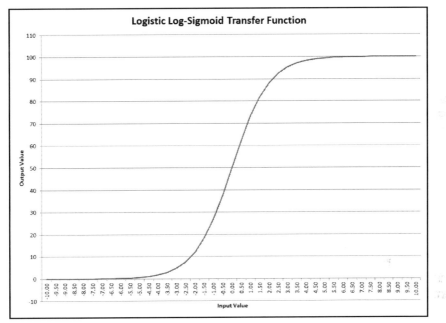

Figure 3.13 -- Logistic function

Entries

Given an entry signal, the entry happens at some *time*, such as the open or the close, or at some *price*, such as a limit order or a stop order.

Time

The pattern is recognized or condition met sometime during the bar. For example, the signal is announced at or after the close of the bar. The entry takes place unconditionally (without restriction to price) at:
- The close of the bar or day that generated the signal. MOC. Market-on-Close.
- The open of the next day. NDO. Next Day Open.
- The close of the next day. As when trading mutual funds.

Price

The pattern is recognized and the signal generated at some specific price.

If the entry signal to a long position is associated with a higher price, the type of order placed with the broker is a "stop" order. For example, pre-compute the price, X, for the intra-day price that exceeds the highest of the previous five closing prices. Then place an order to "Buy at X, stop." If the intra-day price rises above X, the order will be filled at X or worse.

If the entry signal is associated with a lower price, the type of order placed is a "limit" order. For example:
*   Precompute the closing price, W, that would cause the 3 day RSI to be below 20. Be prepared to enter a long position at the close if the closing price is W or lower using a Market On Close, Limit On Close, or Limit order.
*   Precompute the intra-day price, X, that would cause the 5 day z-score using the sequence CCCCX to be below -1.0. Place an order to "buy at X, limit" to enter a long position intra-day if the price drops to X.

The price at which an indicator will have a given value can be pre-computed for almost any of the indicators we use. The requirements are:
*   The computation depends on a single independent variable, usually price. This can be relaxed in some circumstances.
*   The range of indicator values that are computed includes the desired specific value.
*   The relationship is mathematically a function. For any given value of the independent variable, there is one and only one value of the indicator.

When using traditional platforms, the details of price and / or time are specified in the trading system code. When using machine learning, the details are defined in the target used for training.

The technique for anticipating signals is described in detail in my Quantitative Technical Analysis book[6].

Exits

Once in a trade, there are five methods to exit. They are:
*   Logic
*   Profit target
*   Holding period
*   Trailing exit
*   Maximum loss

---

6   Bandy, Howard, *Quantitative Technical Analysis*, Blue Owl Press, 2015.

The model can have rules for any number of them, for all of them, or even for several of a specific method. Whichever rule is satisfied first causes the exit. Good modeling and simulation practice requires that each rule included in the model be used enough times to give statistically significant metrics of its effectiveness.

In pseudo-code, the entry and exit portion of the traditional model have this form:

1. Initialize to no signals.

```
Buy = 0;
Sell = 0;
```

2. Buy and sell is typically based on logic, rules, indicators, and parameters.

```
Buy = LogicBuy;
Sell = LogicSell;
```

3. Sell based on one or more of the exit methods

```
Sell = LogicSell OR ProfitSell OR HoldingPeriodSell
        OR TrailingSell OR MaximumLossSell;
```

Each sell condition is checked each bar, and is set to True when the conditions for it are met. The first in time to be "hit" causes an exit. If two or more become True at the same time, such as at the open of trading or at the close of trading, assume the worst case.

When using machine learning, the details are defined in the target used for training.

Logic

Rules that recognize a pattern. Just as some pattern that precedes a price rise signaled entry, there may be a pattern that precedes a price drop that can be used to signal an exit. The exit rule does not need to be symmetric, or even to use the same indicator as the entry rule. For example, the entry might be signalled by a low RSI, the exit by a moving average cross.

Profit target

Exit at a pre-computed price that results in a profit. The profit target can be a fixed percentage, such as 0.5% (or, for futures, a fixed number of points or dollars), or determined by volatility, such as $1.5 * ATR(3)$. For a long position, the profit target exit is above the entry and is a limit order.

Profit targets work well for systems expecting to hold trades for a short period of time, where large gains are not expected.

Holding period

This method includes timed exits and inactivity exits. Either:
- The number of days (or bars) is determined before or immediately after entry. The trade is exited unconditionally, using an order such as Market on Close, after holding the specified number of bars.
- The profit or loss is analyzed while the trade is open, and a decision based on price action or profit of recent bars is made to exit the trade at the close (or open) of some day. The order is typically a market order for execution at the open (MOO) or at the close (MOC).

Holding periods work well for systems expecting to hold trades for a short period of time, where large gains are not expected.

Trailing exit

A trailing exit requires calculation of a separate price series—call it "trailing price." At trade entry to a long position, the initial trailing price, lower than the entry price, is calculated, and assigned to the entry bar for use during the next bar. At the completion of each bar, a new trailing price is calculated, stored, and ready for reference during the next bar. The new trailing price is never lower than the previous value. Typically, it rises when the primary price rises and profit increases, and it stops rising, or at least slows the rate of rising, when the price stops rising and profit stops increasing.

The idea for the trailing exit is pretty simple:

```
If (Long)
   If (Low < TrailingPrice)  Exit
   Else   Adjust TrailingPrice
Else
   If (Buy)  Initialize TrailingPrice
   Else   Continue Flat
```

Execution is via a stop order. There may be slippage.

There are two commonly used trailing exit algorithms:
- For the *chandelier* version, imagine the trailing price hanging from the primary data series—a chandelier hanging from the ceiling. Either the high or the close can be used as the ceiling. Typically, the distance between the ceiling and the trailing price is a function of bar-to-bar volatility, such as standard deviation or average true range (ATR). The idea is to leave enough distance so that regularly experienced random price variation does not cause an exit, but a significant price drop associated with the end of the trend does cause an exit.
- For the *parabolic* version, the trailing exit begins below some recent price considered to be safely below one day of random price change. With each passing day, the trailing exit price

moves upward. If the price moves upward quickly, the trailing price follows quickly. If the upward movement of the primary price stagnates, the trailing price continues to move upward, but more slowly. Figure 3.14 shows the chart of primary price with the parabolic trailing price. Examine it carefully. The profit or loss is between the buy and sell arrows, not between the initial parabolic and final parabolic.

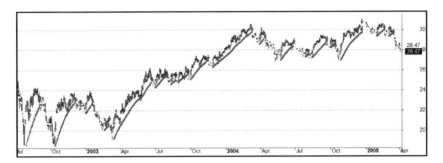

Figure 3.14 Parabolic trailing exit

With either algorithm, eventually the trailing price series and the primary data series will cross as the trailing price rises and / or the primary price falls. The exit takes place intra-bar (intra-day) as a stop order. Each day, or bar, the unexecuted previous exit order is cancelled and replaced with a new order, good for one bar, with a new exit price.

Trailing exits require several bars for the trailing price to catch up to the primary price. If both the primary data series and trailing prices are the same periodicity, trailing exits do not work well for trades held a small number of bars. Alternatively, trailing prices can be based on intra-day bars. Managing a trade where the trailing exit is based on intra-day bars requires action throughout the day as orders are cancelled and replaced.

Maximum loss exit

This is the infamous *money stop*. A stop order is placed some distance below the entry price, hoping to prevent catastrophic loss.

A maximum loss exit seldom improves performance. That is not to say that your system should not have a maximum loss exit. It may be required for customer relations or for regulatory compliance. It is to say that you should expect performance to degrade when one is added.

Test your specific system with the following experiment. Develop the system with any entry and exit rules, but not including a maximum loss exit. Measure performance. Add a maximum loss exit with the exit distance so far below the entry price that it is never used. Make a series of test runs, gradually shortening the exit distance with each successive run. At each, measure performance. My experience is that the tighter the exit, the more the performance degrades.

Having a maximum loss exit rule in a system guarantees that any trade with a maximum adverse excursion at least as great as the loss level will be a losing trade. These trades will never have an opportunity to recover. Like any of the other exits, sound modeling principles require that this technique be the actual reason for trade exit enough times to show statistical significance.

Backtesting and Optimization

Backtesting is the process of fitting the model to the data and observing the resulting performance.

While the word is optimize, the process is:
1. Choose some, usually many, alternative system configurations.
2. Run each as a single run backtest, evaluating the objective function for each, and entering the result into a list.
3. Sort the list according to objective function score.

Choosing alternatives is easy.

The intelligence is in the objective function used to assign each of the alternatives a score so they can be sorted into the order you prefer them.

Discussions of optimization should focus on the objective function, stationarity, and validation. All other aspects of optimization follow from those.

The alternatives are different systems distinguished by having different rules, indicators, and / or parameter values.

For example, if a model is based on the crossing of two moving averages, we want to know the best lengths.

Begin by assigning a value to each length—say 10 and 20. For a single backtest run, the platform computes the value of each moving average for each day. Those days where the two moving averages cross define impulse signals. The platform makes trades using the signals, reports the trade list, computes and reports performance statistics for the model based on crossing the 10 day moving average with the 20 day. The value of the objective function for this pair (10 and 20) is computed.

To find the best pair of moving average lengths, create a list with many pairs of numbers, one number for the length of each moving average, for the range of values desired.

A series of backtests is made, one test for each pair on the list, using the lengths set to the values listed. As each test is completed, the objective function score for that pair is recorded. After all the tests have been run, the list is sorted by objective function score. The best test is at the top of the list, and we note the best lengths for the two moving averages.

Dimensions in a Search Space

The optimization is a search through a *search space*. Each indicator (or other feature being searched) defines a dimension in a search space. In this example, there are two indicators, each with one parameter—length. They define a two-dimensional search space. One dimension is associated with the length of the first moving average. The second dimension is associated with the second moving average.

The values of the lengths being tested can be visualized as being on the x and y axes of a two-dimensional graph. Vertical and horizontal lines define a grid. Each intersection represents one specific ATS with those two specific lengths.

As the backtests are run, a value for each on the objective functions is computed and associated with one of the grid intersections. A contour-like plot connecting points of equal objective function values can be created. It looks like a typographical map, and is called a response surface. Figure 3.15 shows an example. The objective function value is represented on the z-axis. We are searching for the highest stable area of that surface.

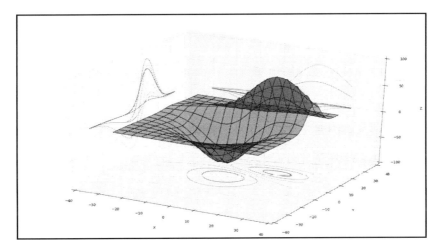

Figure 3.15 Response surface for two-dimensional search space

Each of the dimensions has a list of values to be tested. It is common, but not necessary, for the values to be equally spaced over some range. A moving average might be tested for all integer lengths from 1 to 20. There are 20 values to search in this dimension.

The designer of the model might want the second moving average to be a multiple of ten, between 10 and 100. (Perhaps in an attempt to avoid overfitting, or perhaps to shorten run times while doing preliminary explorations.) There are 10 values to search in this dimension.

The number of points in the search space is the product of the number of points in each of the dimensions. This search space has 200 points. Each represents one of the ATSs being considered.

The search can be expanded to include other indicators, such as the lookback length used to compute an oscillator, and the level at which the oscillator gives a signal.

Each indicator adds a dimension to the search space. Searching for the best combination of two moving averages, an oscillator lookback, and an oscillator critical level is a four-dimensional space. If there are 10 values for the lookback length and 20 values for the critical level, the search space expands from 200 points to 40,000 points.

Global Optimum

Some response surfaces, such as the one shown in Figure 3.14, have a single "mountain" that rises above the "plain." The alternative associated with the grid location of the top of that mountain is the undisputed best. Sometimes there is a single tall hill and several smaller hills. An undisputed tallest hill has the highest objective function score and is the global optimum. The other hills are local optima. Figure 3.16 shows an example.

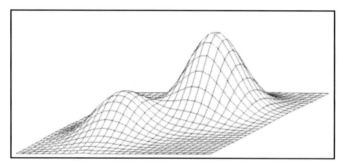

Figure 3.16 A global optimum and one local optimum

Exhaustive Search

An exhaustive search runs a backtest for each and every point in the search space. Since every grid location is tested and scored, an exhaustive search is guaranteed to find the global optimum. When the number of tests is small, execution time is short, and exhaustive searches are preferred.

Non-exhaustive Search

A non-exhaustive search runs fewer backtests than the number of points in the search space. It will still compute an objective function score for each test run, sort them, and choose the highest one as the optimum. The risk is that a poor search algorithm, combined with a poor starting point, may result in the global optimum being missed, with the best found being a local optimum.

Fortunately, there are several algorithms that perform intelligent, non-exhaustive searches that will shorten the computation time considerably while being reasonably certain of finding the global optimum. One that receives good reviews from professional mathematicians, works well in practice, and is available in some trading system development platforms, including AmiBroker, is *covariance matrix adaptation evolution strategy (CMA-ES)*.[7][8]

One of the very big advantages of non-exhaustive searches is that increasing the search space does not increase search time in proportion to the increase in tests requested.

Things to Watch For

If run times are acceptable, use exhaustive search. But search spaces are often so large that exhaustive searches are too lengthy. In that case, use CMA-ES.

Check for spikes in the response surface. Preferred solutions are located in "plateaus" with smooth slopes. The data series will change over time (non-stationarity), changing the performance of the system and the location of the optimum parameter values. If the optimum being traded is on an isolated spike of good performance, it will take only a small change in the characteristics of the data for performance to fall off rapidly.

Check the value returned as optimal for each of the variables being optimized. Unless you specifically want a rigid limit, be aware when an optimal value is at one of the limits of the range. If you asked for a search over 1 to 10, and the reported optimum is 10, there might be an even better result for values greater than 10.

If the objective function is well behaved, you can do exploratory searching of a large search space piecemeal. Set wide limits for each variable and use non-exhaustive search. Based on the preliminary results, focus on a narrower region. Fix some of the parameter values and op-

---

7   Hansen and Ostermeier, Adapting Arbitrary Normal Mutation
     Distributions in Evolution Strategies: The Covariance Matrix
     Adaptation. *Proceedings of the IEEE International Conference on
     Evolutionary Computation*, pages 312-317, 1996.

8   https://www.lri.fr/~hansen/cmaesintro.html

timize others, then fix some of those identified as optimal and test the ones that had been fixed. Repeat for a few iterations. This technique is called evolutionary operation. If the objective function is not well behaved, it may not converge. But it is worth a try.

Do not obsess over perfection. A good local optimum may be satisfactory. Prefer a robust system with lower performance to a fragile system with higher performance.

Optimization and the Curse of Dimensionality

On a forum I regularly follow, a message complained that the trading system development platform the writer was using was unable to handle an optimization that had 10 parameters, each with 20 values. Whether that poster was serious about the numbers 10 and 20 or not, the question is worth considering.

A large number of parameters, say 10, each with a large number of evaluation points, say 20, leads directly to the "curse of dimensionality." Assuming that it takes one nanosecond to evaluate each alternative, and that everything works as it should and the run does finish (no power failure, memory failure, CPU failure, hard disk failure, flood, earthquake, premature death, etc), exhaustive evaluation of the n = 10^20 points will have taken about 3100 years. At 50 lines per 12 inch page, the listing of the results will be 65 light years long. (The nearby universe is described as being those bodies within about 15 light years.)

Each result gives the value of an objective function. Sorting the results into ascending or descending order according to the value of the objective function puts the set of values that are "best" at the top of the list. Assuming a sorting algorithm that takes Order $(n*\ln(n))$ is used, it will take an additional 46 times 3100 years to sort them.

Now make an individual run using each of the sets of values near the top to gain some confidence that the alternative ranked first is the one that is preferred. Maybe an hour or two more?

Just in time to give a signal for tomorrow's trade?

Number of Alternatives to Evaluate

I recommend beginning by giving a considerable amount of thought and experimentation to design and testing of the objective function. Have confidence that the alternative with the highest objective function score is the one that is preferred. Or at least that it is acceptable—not letting the search for perfect get in the way of finding a satisfactory solution.

Run some tests using your system, your objective function, your data, on your computer. How long does it take to generate and sort 1000 or 10,000 alternatives? How many of these test runs do you expect to make before deciding on the logic and parameters that will be used? How many hours are you willing to allocate to the process? Working the arithmetic backwards will give an estimate of the number of alternatives that can realistically be tested. Continuing to work backward, you can compute the size of the parameter space that can be exhaustively processed in that amount of time. Make some trial runs using both exhaustive and non-exhaustive methods. Compare the results that rank best from each set of runs. Decide whether you can accept the results of the non-exhaustive method. If so, use it; if not, modify the code so that the number of parameters and number of evaluation points for each create an examination space that can be processed in the time you have allocated.

Validation

No rational person would trade an untested system. The extremes of the previous example aside, you will want to test several alternatives in order to find the best. Or at least the best within some range of criteria. Be aware that in the process of defining and testing many alternatives, you will create models that fit not the signals, but rather the noise — the idiosyncracies of the data. The problem is that you will not know whether your model has fit to the signal or the noise.

Validation is required to estimate future risk and profit potential. Without independent validation—out-of-sample results showing profitable trades with acceptable risk—there can be no assurance that the model has learned. For the time series systems we are developing, validation means test of the system using data that is both:

• Never used for model adjustment.
• More recent than was used for learning.

This is a high bar.

The caution about data never before used is serious. We all make many changes, modifications, and adjustments to the model as we observe the results of testing. A dangerous time in system development is when we are close to completion of development, making a validation test run, observing something in the results that we would like to be different, and making a tiny adjustment to the model. In that one simple act, the previously out-of-sample data has become in-sample data. The previous test run we intended to be validation is just another backtest. Additional validation data and a fresh test are required to estimate future performance.

The caution about the test data being more recent is equally important. Whenever any system—yours or even one developed and executed by a complete stranger and unknown to you—takes the same trades as yours, that removes some of the inefficiency you are trading. It becomes more difficult to separate the signal from the noise in more recent data, and trades are less profitable. Testing on data earlier than the development data might be interesting, but it has no value as validation.

Walk Forward Testing

The gold standard of validation is walk forward testing. Figures 3.17 through 3.20 illustrate the process.

Walk forward is a sequence of steps. Each step consists of finding the best model using the in-sample data, then using that model to test the out-of-sample data.

Earlier testing and experimentation has determined the hyperparameter associated with stationarity—the length of the in-sample and out-of-sample periods.

The search for the best model is an optimization that tests many alternative models, sorting them into order by objective function score, and choosing the one that is highest ranked. It is important to have confidence that the objective function used ranks alternatives into the same order you subjectively prefer them. Or, at least, you have confidence that the one ranked at the top is satisfactory. During the walk forward process, the choice is made automatically—you do not have an opportunity to evaluate the top choice or any other. It is automatically chosen and applied to the out-of-sample data. The results for the out-of-sample test are stored.

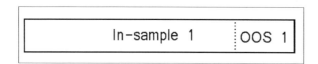

Figure 3.17 A single walk forward step

The process is repeated several times. After each step, the beginning and ending dates of both periods are stepped forward by the length of the out-of-sample period.

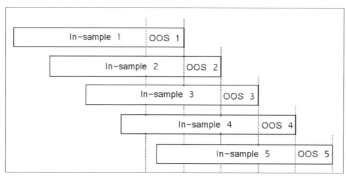

Figure 3.18 A sequence of walk forward steps

The results from all of the out-of-sample tests are accumulated and analyzed. This set of trades is the "best estimate" set of trades. The decision to pass the system forward to trading or return it to development is based on analysis of these trades. See Figure 3.1.

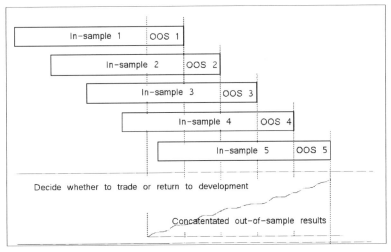

Figure 3.19 Accumulate all the out-of-sample results

If the system is passed on to trading, the process continues. Periodically, either according to the walk forward schedule, or whenever trading results are deteriorating, resynchronize the model to the data using the same process. Take live trades with the most recent model.

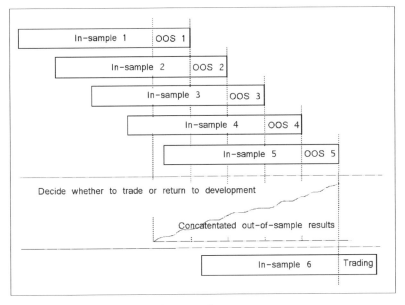

Figure 3.20 Walking forward into trading

These conditions are required for walk forward to work:
- The system is stationary for the combined length of the in-sample and out-of-sample periods.
- You have confidence that the model selected by your objective function as best based on in-sample optimization is satisfactory.
- There are several, preferably many, trades in each test period.

Try to make it work.
- It is a testing process that is very similar to the way the model will be adjusted and the system managed during live trading.
- The set of trades produced by the out-of-sample tests are the best estimate of future performance.

What if walk forward fails to work?
- One, or more, of the conditions do not hold. Try to determine why.
- If the process failed in walk forward testing, do you have confidence that it will work any better when the out-of-sample period is live trading?

There are so many choices. So few are tradable.

There is always a *best*. It is not always tradable. Even when it is, it may not be good enough.

Even Walk Forward Can Fool You

You will probably perform a few walk forward runs before you are satisfied with your system and pass it on to trading. But the same risk of discovering, intentionally or not, a fit to the noise rather than to the signal does exist. As the number of walk forward runs performed increases, the probability of finding a curve-fit solution increases as well.

Chapter 4 — Summary and Important Concepts

Abandon Financial Astrology

Maybe astrology helps with your personal relationships. But whenever some suggests that I incorporate Gann, Fibonacci, or moon phase, I ask for precise definitions that do not repaint, then require thorough testing. None of these have yet passed my filters.

Accuracy

Have a high accuracy ratio for your trades. Keep it above 65%. Below that risk increases dramatically, and risk-normalized profit potential drops.

Also, determining the health of an accurate system is much easier than a system with low accuracy.

And it is much easier psychologically to trade a system that has a high rate of winning trades.

Algorithms

Algorithms are more accurate in prediction than human experts.

Are We Predicting?

Yes. Definitely. Every trade made is a prediction of a change in price.

Backtest

No matter how steep and smooth an in-sample backtest looks—whether it is the plot of the equity curve or the statistical summary—it has no value in estimating future performance. An unbiased validation using data more recent in the series and not previously tested is required.

Become a Competent Programmer

You must be able to design, program, debug, and operate your own programs. Do not rely on a black box or a consultant.

Best Estimate

If the data used to populate the best estimate set is badly biased, then augmented by realized trades, the distribution is a mixture of two different processes. The result is more uncertain than if the prior is assumed to be random.

Bad data is worse than no data.

CAR25

CAR25 is a universal objective function. It is the estimated growth rate of the trading system, normalized for risk.

Check List

A check list of the tasks of trading system development.

- A system is a model plus data. Refer to the section "Every Model-Data Combination is a System," in Chapter 1. Pick one cell and work with it.
- Select an issue to trade. Refer to the technique and list in the section "What the Prospector Found," in Chapter 2. Pick one. If the system is not successful, try a different one. But work with one at a time.
- Define your personal risk tolerance. See the section "Risk Tolerance," in Chapter 1.
- Fill in the settings for your trading account. Define the amount of funds you want to commit to trading this system, whether you plan to be long/flat or short/flat, brokerage commissions, and so forth.
- Decide when you will be gathering data, evaluating the system, generating signals, and entering trades.
- Decide what kind of trades you want to make—market on close, limit order, etc.
- Decide what objective function will be used. Refer to the section "CAR25—Universal Objective Function," in Chapter 1. If the platform you will be using supports CAR25, use it. If not, refer to the section "Alternative Objective Functions," in Chapter 3.
- Decide the characteristics of the signals and trades you will be searching for. If you are using impulse signals, these are the Buy and Sell signals (assuming you are trading long/flat). If you are using state signals, these are the one-day-ahead changes of state.
- Choose one or more indicators. An indicator is a data transformation. The frequency of signals will correspond with the frequency of changes of the indicators. If you want two

signals each week, the indicators chosen must change in an important and predictive way two times each week.

- Backtest and optimize. Search for the model that best fits the data. Best is measured by your objective function. The backtest, adjust, retest cycle can be very extensive. You will probably define and test thousands of alternative models to arrive at the final system.
- Validate that the model that best fits the in-sample data does represent a general fit, not just a fit to the specific in-sample data. Without successful validation, there can be no confidence.

Curse of Dimensionality

Limit the number of parameters.

The symbol space is a parameter.

Data Is What It Is

Financial data does not follow Normal distribution. Do not assume that it does, nor try to force it to be, nor naively use techniques that assume Normality.

Data Prospector

Listen to the Data Prospector. He holds the key to your kingdom. Unless the data series you plan to trade passes his filters, there is no model that works. You will not be able to develop a low-risk profitable system.

Degree of Belief

When a gambling analyst tells us that the probability of the ball landing in a red pocket of a fair roulette wheel is 18 out of 38, or 47.4%, that probability can be verified experimentally with repeated trials. As the number of trials grows very large and approaches infinity, the proportion of those trials where the outcome was red approaches 47.4%. This is a frequentist interpretation of probability.

When a political analyst predicts a 65% probability of a candidate winning, the 65% value is not the result of repeating an experiment many times and counting the proportion where she won. It is a statement of the degree of belief that she will win.

From the frequentist perspective, the data is seen as random with fixed parameters to be estimated. Sampling is infinite, and decision rules can be sharp. Studies can be repeated. There is no information prior to the specification of the model.

From the Bayesian perspective, the data is seen as given. The parameters are unknown and random, and are updated as additional data is observed. Studies cannot be repeated. Prior information is important and useful.

Use whichever tools are helpful in solving the problem or establishing the confidence you need.

Discard Harmful Biases

Nostalgia is fine for antique furniture. But not for techniques for trading.

Distributions

Understand and use cumulative distribution functions and their charts.

Black swans live in the tails of distributions of risk.

Embrace Monte Carlo

Understand and use Monte Carlo simulation and analysis to study relationships and alternatives. Be aware of requirements and assumptions.

Enough

When You Have Enough, Quit

No matter how profitable, consistent, and safe your system appears, there is always a non-zero probability of an account destroying black swan event.

Equity Curve

As system development continues, for a given period of time the systems tested draw their trades from the same population. Some of the equity curves you see are poor, and you ignore those. Some are good because the model does identify profitable signals. Some are good because of a lucky fit to the noise in the data. Every good equity curve is optimistic. Complete the validation and the risk-normalized profit estimate before considering trading.

Expectation

No rational person would trade a system that has a negative expectation. If, for some reason, you must bet where the odds are against you, be bold. A series of many small bets is guaranteed to lose. Instead, make a few large bets, then win or lose, walk away.

Think roulette. Betting red / black guarantees a loss. Betting a single number has a low probability of a win, but a high payoff if it does win. If you enter a casino with $100 intent on increasing your bankroll, plan to make ten $10 bets on your favorite lucky number. Quit ater the first win.

Feature Engineering

A simple algorithm with refined data usually outperforms a complex algorithm with raw data.

Gambling

Trading systems are not like roulette. Roulette has no model that works.

Trading systems are like blackjack. There is a model that works under some conditions. We want to recognize the conditions and play correctly. Stand aside otherwise.

Hard! This is So Hard!

You are competing one-on-one with Goldman Sachs. There are no handicaps and no mulligans.

Holding Period

The sweet spot is one or two days. The longer the holding period, the lower the risk-normalized profit.

Impartial Goal

List all subjective constraints, planning to exclude any system that violates any of them.

Consider all remaining systems impartially. Normalize for risk, then use those that have the highest account growth.

Is It Broken?

Make certain you can tell when your system performance is deteriorating. Take drawdowns as early warnings to reduce position size.

Kahneman

Read Daniel Kahneman, *Thinking, Fast and Slow*.

Learning and Model Complexity

Training data
- Guide the learning
- In-sample

Testing data
- Test whether learning happened
- Out-of-sample

Learning

- The model fits the training data, and also gives accurate predictions for test and live data.

Overfitting
- The model fits the training data, but gives inaccurate predictions for out-of-sample data.
- Make the model less complex, or replace it.

Not learning
- The model does not fit the training data. (Hence, cannot be trusted no matter how it fits the out-of-sample data.)
- Make the model more complex, or replace it.

Long / Flat

Work with systems that trade a single issue long / flat.

Luck and Skill

Outcomes of most activities depend on both luck and skill, with examples at both ends of that spectrum. Compare roulette, which is 100% luck, with chess, which is 100% skill. The higher the skill component, the lower the chance that a novice will win over an expert.

Machine Learning

Study machine learning. Your competition already is.

Mantra

Mantra—a set of often repeated phrases that expresses basic beliefs.

My mantra is simple:
- Select data series that offer adequate profit without excessive risk.
- Use the scientific method to develop a rule-based model.
- Include rules for all actions.
- Use state-based signals.
- Synchronize monitoring the system with managing the system.
- Have a positive expectation.
- Trade frequently.
- Trade accurately.
- Hold a short period of time.
- Avoid serious losses.
- Monitor trade-by-trade results and adjust position size as performance changes.

Together, these give confidence that your trading account will grow and have low risk of account destroying drawdown. Failing any one of these is enough to risk loss of your trading account.

Mathematics

You must understand the mathematics that is the foundation of both trading systems and trading management. You must be able to assess program operation and results.

Model

The entire and only purpose of the model is to identify the signals that precede profitable trades.

Model and Data

We are fitting a model to data so we can use the model to make predictions. Our first prediction is the direction of price change. Our confidence in that prediction is expressed in the size of the position taken.

Nothing is Stationary

Nothing about financial data or trading systems is stationary.

Every tool and technique you use must deal with changes in relationships.

Physical Laws

There are no physical laws governing the behavior of financial markets. If there were, new information would not matter much, and there would be little profit opportunity.

Portfolios

Modern portfolio theory is based on a backward looking model with assumptions of stationarity, and often allows the infinite parameter space of all stocks. If you must build a system that takes positions in more than a single issue, select the issues in advance and be certain each is held for enough days to be significant.

It is much more difficult to validate a portfolio than a system that trades a single issue.

Position Sizing

Should not be in the trading system.

Should be in the trading management system.

Precision and Accuracy

Precision in-sample does not assure accuracy out-of-sample.

Prediction

Are we predicting? Yes! The model is identifying, in advance, profitable trading opportunities. It is predicting them.

Psychology

Begin with your preferences. Define your own objective functions.

No cognitive dissonance $\Longrightarrow$ no need for a psychology to help you feel good about trading a system that does not fit you.

Quantify Your Risk Tolerance

I am trading a $100,000 account, and forecasting two years. I want to hold the probability of a drawdown greater than 20% to a chance of 5%.

Use your risk tolerance to normalize results for comparison.

Read, Read, Read

This field is changing with astonishing speed. Subscribe to discussion forums, read research journals, watch lectures. Stay current. Your competition is.

Regime Switching

Absent reasons not related to the performance, CAR25 can be used to rank alternative systems in a regime switching *portfolio of systems*.

Risk
- Personal
- Data
- System

Scientific Method

The scientific method is a sequence of steps:
- Data mine in-sample to learn, typically iterating many times. Pick rules and parameters to identify patterns and generate buy and sell signals.
- Validate the model by testing out-of-sample data.

Short / Flat

When the long / flat system works, try short / flat. For issues that are not symmetric in price changes up and down, such as equities, it will be harder to find good models for short trades. Bottoms have better definition than tops. There is an upward bias to the price of equities.

The short / flat model does not need to be the inverse of the long / flat model—in fact that seldom works. Choose other indicators and parameters.

Signal to Noise

The ratio is low. Be extra vigilant that your system recognizes the signal. That it is not merely fit to the noise.

Small safe-f

The value of safe-f is related to the expected drawdown in the entire account trading the system—both the portion in shares and the portion in ballast funds. If the value of safe-f that is returned by the dynamic position sizing algorithm is small, drawdowns in the portion that is in the market will be much larger than your stated tolerance.

This much larger: 1.00 / safe-f.

State-Based Signals

Better resolution than impulse-based signals. Better trade management.

Stationarity

Nothing is stationary.
- Not prices.
- Not detrended prices.
- Not differenced prices.
- Not volatility.
- Not indicator signal frequency.
- Not distribution of signals.
- Not distribution of trades.
- Not trade frequency.
- Not trade profitability.
- Not position size.

Deal with the non-stationarity. Treating financial data and trading systems with tools that assume stationarity guarantees failure.

System Evaluation

Given two systems, compare them by normalizing the risk, then comparing the annual rate of growth. Does anything else matter?

Think Bayes

Think probabilistically.

You do not need 30 bites to know to avoid the dog.

Toxic Trades

Avoiding bad trades is more important than finding good ones.

Trade Management

Mark to market daily. Manage daily.

Trend Following

The phrase "trend following" is used in several contexts.
1. An entry technique. The pattern being recognized is that
    the price has been in a trend according to some trendiness
    indicator. A signal to enter a position is generated. The reason
    a trading system would use this entry is the expectation that
    the trend will continue. Test this as you would any indicator
    and rule.
2. A trading philosophy. Trend following is a euphemism for
    holding positions for a long time anticipating large gains.
    This falls into the category of conventional wisdom. The
    technique was very successful through the 1980s and early
    90s. As the markets have become more efficient, the profit per
    time period has decreased and intra-trade risk increased. Pay
    careful attention to the risk. Select a set of trades that you feel
    are representative and work through the risk / safe-f / CAR25
    calculations.
3. Every trade. Every trade is a trend following trade for the
    period it is held. To be profitable, the sell price must be higher
    than the buy price—a trend.

TWR = G ^ N

TWR: Terminal Wealth Relative.

G: Have a positive expectation.

N: Trade frequently.

Conclusion and Recommendation

Begin with these recommendations and modify to suit your conditions and preferences.

- Read Daniel Kahneman's book, "Thinking, Fast and Slow."
- Define your personal risk tolerance statement.
- Include all trading rules as formulas in your model.
- Use CAR25 as your objective function.
- Trade a single issue long / flat.
- Pick an issue that passes the data prospector's two filters:
    * Enough volatility to provide some profit potential.
    * Not so much volatility that no system will be safe.
- Use state signals.
- Mark-to-market daily.
- Select a small number of indicators.
- Tune the indicator(s) to give signals at the same frequency you want trades.
- The sweet spot is:
    * Trade accurately—65% correct or better.
    * Hold a short period—one or two days.
- Have a positive expectation.
- Trade frequently.
- Pick a model paradigm, such as decision tree. Consider others.
- Do some exploratory system tests.
- Determine the length of stationarity.
- Pick a length for in-sample.
- Pick a length for out-of-sample.
- Use the scientific method:
    * Fit the model to the data in-sample.
    * Validate there is generalization out-of-sample.
- Use walk forward testing to validate.
- Use several OOS periods and create a best estimate set of trades.
- Compute safe-f for best estimate set of trades.
- At safe-f, compute CAR25 for best estimate set.
- Decide whether the system is worth trading.
- Apply dynamic position sizing trade-by-trade to manage trading and determine system health.

If You Do Not Believe It

The response to the conclusions and recommendations expressed in the book is sometimes disbelief. They are contrary to conventional wisdom. They require knowledge and skill in three areas:
- Domain expertise—the markets.
- Programming—ability to design, program, debug, and operate the computer programs needed.
- Mathematics—ability to understand the math, probability, and statistics. I recommend math through calculus and linear algebra.

It exposes the difficulties:
- Low signal to noise ratio.
- Stiff competition.
- Nearly efficient market.
- Low risk-normalized profit potential.
- Steep learning curve.

It questions conventional wisdom:
- Trend following, as in long holding for a small proportion of high profit trades is a good technique.
- Systems are stationary.
- Backtest results are indicative of future performance.
- Profit is more important than risk.
- Every model should work for every tradable issue.
- Position sizing calculations belong in the model.
- Portfolios are better than individual issues.
- The best indicators have long lookbacks and change slowly.
- Long holding periods are best.
- Infrequent historical events are predictive.
- It is OK to revise previous indicators and signals.

It is possible that whatever methods you are using now are better than the one I suggest. Begin by applying the scientific method. Compute the risk-normalized estimate of compound annual growth to the out-of-sample results of whichever systems you are contemplating using.

Appendix A — Fundamental Analysis

In order to be valuable, any data series or indicator, company data or economic series, must be:
* Timely
* Accurate
* Predictive

There are several issues that complicate use of fundamental economic or company data for trading.
* *Timeliness related to reporting granularity.* Fundamental data is reported annually, quarterly, monthly, or weekly. Trading decisions are made monthly, weekly, daily, or intra-day. If the stock price is reported and acted upon more frequently than the economic indicator is reported, there will be many time periods (data bars) where there is no new data for the economic indicator. In order to have a value to use in calculations, the latest value that does exist will be copied forward until a new value is received. Useful patterns are based on changes in data series. The only time that value can change is on those days when a new report is received.
* *Timeliness related to revision.* Economic indicators, and other fundamental data, are reported, then revised at later dates. When the historical data is retrieved from the data provider, it will usually be a series that consists of only the final revision data. In order to maintain consistency, the data value associated with a given time period cannot be used in the trading system until after the date and time its final revision is published. See Figure A.1, a chart showing the dates associated with the US government GDP report. The GDP report covers the months January, February, and March. The *advance* report is issued at the end of April, the month following the quarter, followed by the *preliminary* report one month later, and the *final* report two months later. In July, the series is *rebased*, adjusting

and changing all previously reported values.

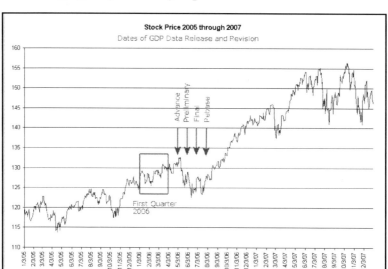

Figure A.1 Revision history of fundamental data

An alternative is to use a series that consists solely of data initially released, with no revisions or adjustments applied. The trading system would then be based on initial release data rather than final release data. For some series, this is workable. For others, not even the signs of the values published in the preliminary and final reports agree.

• *Accuracy related to revision.* Government statistical series are regularly given annual adjustments, are re-based, and re-benchmarked. Re-basing sets a new date for the base of the index (the date it has a value of, say, 100) and adjusts all data in the series accordingly. Re-benchmarking recalculates the relationship between indicator series, adjusting those that depend on others. Any of these operations result in a revised historical data series, potentially changing patterns and signals.

Corporate data has similar problems:

* Before about 1980 revisions and restatements of corporate data were unusual — about 3 of the S&P 500 companies each year. Since 1995, and particularly since 2000, revisions have become much more common — about 80 of the S&P 500 in 2002, and more broadly an average of more than one per company per year.[1]

---

1   Giroux, Gary, *Business Scandals, Corruption, and Reform: An Encyclopedia*, Greenwood, 2013

*   There is the regular use of one-time entries that seriously distort data.
*   Corporate reorganization causes data to be revised.

- *Accuracy related to bias.* There is a bias to any reported data. That bias is unknown, and unknowable, to users of the data. Whether the report is unintentionally biased due to an innocent data preparation error or omission, or intentionally misleading, outsiders probably cannot detect the bias, its amount, or its reason. They have little alternative but to accept and use the data as reported. Bias introduces a systematic error into the reported statistic that lasts as long as that particular bias persists.
- *Accuracy related to measurement.* The fundamental statistic reported is the result of subjective interpretation of reports, questionnaires, and interviews. Preparers of these reports must be careful to avoid confusing precision with accuracy. Measurement introduces a random error into the reported statistic.
- *Degrees of freedom.* There are hundreds of series of economic data that could be chosen. Each series has a limited number of data points. Choosing a series risks selection bias. Fitting rules to the few data points risks overfitting.
- *Predictive.* Whether the fundamental data is predictive depends on the strength of the relationship, the efficiency with which the market assimilates the information, and the insight and skill of the developer of the trading system. Remember to follow good modeling and validation practices. Keep enough data reserved for out-of-sample testing. In-sample results are always good and have no value in predicting the profitability of a system when traded on unseen data.

For all of these reasons, it is difficult to incorporate the fundamental data series with the daily, or even weekly, price series representing the trading prices. An alternative is to find surrogate data series such as indexes, ETFs, stocks, or mutual funds that:

- Reflect changes in the fundamental data.
- Represent transactions made in public and reported through a clearing agency.
- Are reported on the same time schedule as the price series being traded.
- Are never revised.

Inclusion of intermarket data, such as interest rates, can be used for broad market timing, or to create filters to permit or block equity trades.

Surrogate data, primarily in the form of sector indexes defined and maintained by financial services companies, can be useful in active trading systems.

Appendix B — Data Sources

The best situation would be to use the same data for development as for trading. Unfortunately, that is unlikely.

The bid, ask, and execution prices available on your broker's screen are provided by your broker for your convenience. The broker's business is brokerage, not data distribution. Under normal circumstances you can expect a reputable broker to display the best bid and ask and a stream of transaction records in near real time. When there is a resource limitation—such as saturated communications—the brokerage data stream will be reduced to fit the available capacity. The trade history recorded from a single broker is nearly certain to be incomplete and will not agree with the historical trade data downloaded some time after those trades were made.

Be aware of the possible problems associated with broker-supplied data for use in trading system development.

Data supplied by a data service that is not a broker is more likely to be complete, but it cannot be directly traded.

My suggestion is a compromise:
- For development, use high quality data obtained from a source whose stated purpose is to distribute complete and accurate data.
- For trading:
  * Feed your trading system program from the same source used for development.
  * Generate the buy and sell signals from the trading system running in the development platform.
  * Verify on your broker's screen that the broker's quotations are accurate.
  * Place your trades using your broker's utilities.

The sections that follow identify and briefly discuss several sources of price data. Some provide only historical data—end-of-day data some time after the markets close, or intra-day data reported after a delay of some time. Others distribute real-time data, reported as soon after the data was created as possible. Most have a range of products and services at a range of prices, allowing you to select what you need. The completeness of the data provided varies with vendor—do enough research to satisfy yourself that the data provided meets your needs.

All are data vendors, and all are currently in business as this is written. You should expect changes as new vendors enter the business and others drop out. Join the user groups and discussion forums for the platform you use and the data vendors you are using or considering using.

You have some choices to make related to the data you will use for development.

- The source—where the data will come from.
    * Free.
    * Subscription.
- Database location.
    * Locally, on your own computer.
    * On the data server's computer, downloading what you need when you need it.
- Database maintenance.
    * The data vendor corrects errors and adjusts for splits and distributions. (In most cases, you are unable to make modifications to the vendor-maintained database.)
    * You maintain the database.

csi
http://www.csidata.com/

End-of-day historical data for US and Canadian stocks, world futures, Forex, indexes, government rates, ETFs, mutual funds. Subscription. Data is stored on your computer in a proprietary format. Data is maintained by the vendor.

dtn.iq
http://www.interquote.com/

Real-time, tick-by-tick streaming data for stocks, futures, options. Subscription. Your software requires a "client process" to receive the quotes, functions to interpret the data, and functions to store it to your local database (if you want to record the data for future use).

eoddata
http://www.eoddata.com/

End-of-day and one minute-based intra-day data for stocks, ETFs, mutual funds, commodities on markets around the world. A limited amount is available free, most require a subscription. Data is downloaded to your computer and stored in one of a number of formats, including ASCII, MetaStock, and several specific to trading system development platforms.

eSignal
`http://www.esignal.com/`

Real-time, tick-by-tick, streaming data for stocks, futures, options. Subscription. Uses eSignal and third-party software.

Google
`https://www.google.com/finance`

End-of-day historical data for stocks, indexes, mutual funds for US and many world markets. Real-time data for stocks using beta-test data feed. Free. API procedures for direct feed to your application are available for many development platforms. Or download in csv format and store in your local database.

Interactive Brokers
`https://www.interactivebrokers.com/ind/en/main.php`

A broker whose data service is high quality. End-of-day and intra-day historical, and real-time streaming, data through the TWS (Trader Work Station). Some free, some subscription. Download in csv format and store in your local database. Direct access to live trading applications through the TWS API.

msn money
`http://money.msn.com/`

End-of-day historical data for stocks, indexes, mutual funds for US and many world markets. Free. Download in csv format and store in your local database.

nasdaq
`http://www.nasdaq.com/quotes/historical-quotes.aspx`

End-of-day data for stocks and ETFs listed on the all US exchanges. Free. Download historical data in csv format. Intra-day prices, including pre-market and after-hours, are available for view—some real-time, some with 20 minute delay. Historical commodity prices viewable but not downloadable.

Norgate Premium Data
`http://www.premiumdata.net/`

End-of-day historical data for stocks, futures, Forex for US and many world markets. Subscription. Vendor maintains a database (in several formats including MetaStock, ASCII, and the preferred proprietary) on your computer, updating content with each download. Extensive historical data, including survivorship adjusted data, is available.

Quandl
`http://www.quandl.com/`

A large number of end-of-day datasets for global markets, including indexes, commodities, stocks, interest rates. Some free, some subscription. Extensive historical data download in csv, Excel, json, R, or xml format. Free API for direct access of Quandl by AmiBroker, Python, C/C++/C#, Excel, Java, Maple, Matlab, R, Stata, and more. Quandl is a data aggregator and redistributor. Their premium data is available shortly after market close. Intra-day historical data, but not real-time data, is available via subscription.

US Treasury
`www.treasury.gov/`

Daily T-Bill, T-Note, T-Bond, and yield-curve spread rates. Free. Copy and paste to your spreadsheet. Store in your local database.

Yahoo! Finance
`http://finance.yahoo.com/`

End-of-day historical data for stocks, indexes, mutual funds for US and many world markets. Free. API procedures for direct feed to your application are available for many development platforms. Or download in csv format and store in your local database.

Appendix C — Development Platforms

Technical analysts who plot price and volume, inspect the chart, and use their experience and expert judgement to trade, can use one of the many excellent charting packages to prepare their data.

Quantitative technical analysts use precisely defined logical and mathematical expressions to identify signals and trades. Whether simple, such as moving averages, or complex, such as support vector machines using non-linear kernels, the mathematics is invariably implemented as a computer program.

Your success as a quantitative technical analyst depends very much on your ability to understand the mathematics and logic that represent these techniques, and to accurately translate and implement them as computer programs.

There is no alternative. You must understand the techniques and the associated math. You must be able to read, write, and execute computer programs.

Two Approaches

One uses the traditional trading system development platform, computes indicators and identifies patterns, and observes how prices change over the period of time that follows. Call this the *indicator and what follows* approach.

The other uses data science and machine learning. In it, we first identify the trades that have the desired characteristics, then look for persistent patterns that precede those trades. Call this the *notable trade and what precedes it* approach.

Figure C.1 shows the development process and illustrates that the two approaches occupy the same position in the development process. You may decide to do all your development using one platform, or you may decide to use both.

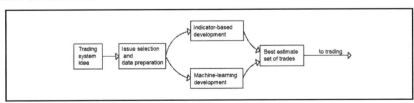

Figure C.1 Two development paths

Trading System Development Platform

For traditional technical analysis, chart-based, and indicator-based systems my choice has long been, and continues to be, AmiBroker. I recommend AmiBroker as being the best available to individuals and small trading companies based on its superior capabilities alone. A nice bonus is its reasonable cost.

AmiBroker is distributed from its website.[1] A free and fully functional trial is available. There is extensive support and reference material on the AmiBroker site. Complete instructions for installing AmiBroker and setting up several sources of data, as well as a set of ten graduated exercises that guide new users through the capabilities of the program, can be found in my book, *Introduction to AmiBroker*,[2] available free in downloadable pdf format.[3]

My earlier books, *Quantitative Trading Systems*,[4] *Mean Reversion Trading Systems*,[5] and *Quantitative Technical Analysis*[6] address the design, testing, and validation of trading systems from the indicator-based perspective. They all use AmiBroker to illustrate and implement the ideas and techniques.

AmiBroker runs under Windows. Both 32 bit and 64 bit operating systems are supported, and AmiBroker itself comes in both 32 bit and 64 bit versions.

All versions of AmiBroker—trial and registered, standard and professional, end-of-day and real-time—begin with a visit to the AmiBroker web site and downloading the installation file. As of this writing, the latest version is 6.10. Click the Download AmiBroker link, choose the 32 bit or 64 bit version, and download the installation file. The file for the 64 bit version is about 9 MB. Save it to your hard disc. Double click the file to begin installation. Accept all defaults.

When the installation is complete, launch AmiBroker. The installation will have created an AmiBroker icon on your desktop. Double-click that. When AmiBroker starts, it displays a message that it is Standard

---

1   https://www.amibroker.com/
2   Bandy, Howard, *Introduction to AmiBroker, Second Edition*, Blue Owl Press, 2012.
3   http://www.introductiontoamibroker.com/
4   Bandy, Howard, *Quantitative Trading Systems, Second Edition*, Blue Owl Press, 2011.
5   Bandy, Howard, *Mean Reversion Trading Systems*, Blue Owl Press, 2013.
6   Bandy, Howard, *Quantitative Technical Analysis*, Blue Owl Press, 2015.

Edition and Unregistered. This is the trial version, but will be instantly converted to Registered (and Professional Edition, if you requested that) when your AmiBroker Registration file is processed. In the mean time, AmiBroker is ready for your use in Trial mode. The installation includes a small database suitable for testing.

The User's Guide is included in the download, is indexed and searchable, and is accessible by pressing the F1 key when in AmiBroker.

Data Science and Machine Learning

For the data science approach, there are literally hundreds of computer languages that could be used. Ideally, the one we use will have these characteristics and capabilities:
* Readily available
* Inexpensive
* Widely supported
* Easily learned
* Flexible input and output
* Flexible display of graphical output
* Efficient at handling financial time series
* Efficient numeric computation
* Efficient matrix computation
* Library of machine learning applications
* Library of statistical analysis applications

As recently as 2010, the choice was not clear, and the solution involved multiple languages and applications packages inefficiently cobbled together. Components typically included, among many others:
* General programming: C++, Java, Visual Basic, Python.
* Financial time series: AmiBroker, TradeStation.
* Statistical analysis: R, SPSS, Stata.
* Scientific library: C, C++, FORTRAN, MATLAB, Excel.

Python was just one of the contenders to be a single-application platform for quantitative analysis.

Python

In 2011, with the publication of *pandas*[7] by Wes McKinney, it became crystal clear that Python had risen to be the top choice. McKinney developed pandas for his own use while a quantitative analyst at AQR Capital Management. Pandas provides several capabilities—most importantly the DataFrame data structure and the set of functions that handle financial time series. His book[8] is essential reading.

---

7 http://pandas.pydata.org/
8 McKinney, Wes, *Python for Data Analysis*, O'Reilly, 2012.

The Python language was developed, beginning in 1989, by Guido van Rossum in the Netherlands. It is open source. It is free. It runs under Windows, Mac OS, UNIX / Linux, and even Raspberry Pi, among others.

It was released to the public in February 1991; Version 2.0 was released in October 2000, and Version 3.0 in December 2008. By design, Python is highly readable and easily programmed. It uses English keywords and indentation to define program structure. It is highly extensible. When I first wrote this paragraph, January 2014, Python was supported by over 38,000 libraries and packages. Currently, July 2016, there are over 84,000 in PyPI alone[9].

Python, with the scientific stack of NumPy, SciPy, pandas, and matplotlib, is exceptionally easy to work with, well supported, powerful, and inexpensive. Many packages, such as scikit-learn, are available to provide classification, regression, dimension reduction, and other modeling and machine learning capabilities. If the analysis requires faster execution, critical routines can be written in compiled languages such as FORTRAN or C++ and linked in transparently. If the analysis requires functions specific to R, MATLAB, or Excel, data can be prepared in Python, processed in those programs, with results returned to Python for further analysis. It meets all of the requirements to be a single-language, data science-based, quantitative technical analysis platform.

The components you will need, all of which are free, are:
* Python—base language
* NumPy—support for multidimensional arrays
* SciPy—modules for scientific computing
* pandas—time series library
* matplotlib—plotting library
* scikit-learn—machine learning

Environments

Your Python environment can be on your machine, or you can use one of the many web-based or cloud-based service providers. Some of the on-line choices are free services whose main application is on-line tutorials, such as:
* Learn Python
  `www.learnpython.org`
* Code Academy
  `www.codeacademy.com`
* Online Python Tutor
  `www.pythontutor.com`

---

9 `https://pypi.python.org/pypi`

Others are powerful cloud-based sites, intended to support always-on computation, such as Python Anywhere

`www.pythonanywhere.com`

And joint-effort program development, such as cloud9

`https://c9.io`

On-line services are easy to use, accessible from any computer, and do not require installation of software on your computer.

Trading system development is computationally intensive, and you will soon reach the limits of the free on-line services provide. Assuming you might want to install a Python development environment on your own computer, there are some excellent alternatives.

In order to make easy use of Wes McKinney's book, I recommend using the operating environment he uses. That is Python version 2.7, iPython, NumPy, SciPy, pandas, and matplotlib.

One reference that stands out is Dr. Allen Downey's book, *Think Python*.[10] It is an introduction to both Python and to computer science. The book is available in print, and also as a free e-book.[11] Downey's website provides downloadable code for programs in his book.[12]

Spyder

Spyder is an open source cross-platform interactive development environment for scientific programming in Python. Spyder integrates Python with the support libraries, a program editor and file manager, and the iPython execution environment. The Spyder website[13] has documentation, including links to several installation options.

Installation

I use and recommend the Continuum Analytics Anaconda implementation of the Python environment. It is free. All of the support libraries we need, as well as Spyder, are installed in a single operation using the default Anaconda installer. Begin with a visit to their website.

`https://store.continuum.io/cshop/anaconda/`

Should you eventually need it, Anaconda supports *Accelerate* and *CUDA*, add-ons for Anaconda that make use of multi-core CPUs and GPUs.

---

10 Downey, Allen, *Think Python*, O'Reilly, 2012.
11 `http://www.greenteapress.com/thinkpython/`
12 `http://www.greenteapress.com/thinkpython/code/`
13 `https://pythonhosted.org/spyder/`

Reference

My *Quantitative Technical Analysis* book includes an introduction to machine learning. It demonstrates how to translate trading systems written in AmiBroker into Python, outlines data preparation for machine learning, and gives complete and ready-to-run code that implements safe-f and dynamic position sizing.

Tutorials

Please read some of the books and visit some of the sites that specialize in Python tutorials. While you do eventually need to become a competent programmer, you can continue reading this book while you practice Python.

Appendix D — Bibliography

The bibliography is intended to be practical rather than encyclopedic. I have listed books and websites that I have found provide background and examples that are helpful in learning about and implementing trading systems with the characteristics that have high probability of being profitable with low risk.

This list is heavy in machine learning, pattern recognition, probability, statistics, modeling, and simulation—because those topics are of primary importance in developing quantitative trading systems. It is light on traditional trading systems, indicators, and charting—because those topics are not very useful for systems that fit the trading profile most likely to be profitable with low risk.

If you can only read one

Kahneman, Daniel, *Thinking, Fast and Slow*, Farrar, Straus, and Giroux, 2011.

But you will need more than one

Abu-Mostafa, Yaser, Malik Magdon-Ismail, and Hsuan-Tien Lin, *Learning from Data*, AML Books, 2012.

—, *Machine Learning*, California Institute of Technology, online course. https://work.caltech.edu/

Aronson, David, and Timothy Masters, *Statistically Sound Machine Learning for Algorithmic Trading of Financial Instruments: Developing Predictive-Model-Based Trading Systems Using TSSB*, Aronson, 2013.

Bandy, Howard, *Introduction to AmiBroker: Advanced Technical Analysis Software for Charting and Trading System Development*, Second Edition, Blue Owl Press, 2012. http://www.introductiontoamibroker.com/

—, *Mean Reversion Trading Systems: Practical Methods for Swing Trading*, Blue Owl Press, 2013.

—, *Modeling Trading System Performance: Monte Carlo Simulation, Position Sizing, Risk Management, and Statistics*, Blue Owl Press, 2011.

—, *Quantitative Technical Analysis: An integrated approach to trading system development and trading management*, Blue Owl Press, 2015.

—, *Quantitative Trading Systems: Practical Methods for Design, Testing, and Validation*, Second Edition, Blue Owl Press, 2011.

—, *The Importance of Being Stationary*, YouTube Video, 2015,
`https://www.youtube.com/watch?v=iBhrZKErJ6A&feature=youtu.be`

—, *The Four Faces of Risk*, YouTube Video, 2015,
`https://www.youtube.com/watch?v=Vw7mseQ_Tmc&feature=youtu.be`

—, *Trading System Development: Indicator-Based*, YouTube Video, 2015,
`https://www.youtube.com/watch?v=W-gSsqHORJE&feature=youtu.be`

—, *Trading System Development: Machine Learning*, YouTube Video, 2015,
`https://www.youtube.com/watch?v=v729evhMpYk&feature=youtu.be`

Bishop, Christopher, *Pattern Recognition and Machine Learning*, Springer, 2007.

—, *Introduction to Bayesian Inference*, video lecture.
`http://videolectures.net/mlss09uk_bishop_ibi/`

Bostrom, Nick, *Superintelligence: Paths, Dangers, Strategies*, Oxford, 2014.

Box, George, and Friends, *Improving Almost Anything: Ideas and Essays*, Revised Edition, Wiley, 2006.

Bressert, Eli, *SciPy and NumPy: An Overview for Developers*, O'Reilly, 2013.

Brownlee, Jason, *Clever Algorithms: Nature-Inspired Programming Recipes*, Brownlee, 2012.

Connors, Larry, and Cesar Alvarez, *High Probability ETF Trading: 7 Professional Strategies to Improve Your ETF Trading*, Connors, 2009.

—, *How Markets Really Work: A Quantitative Guide to Stock Market Behavior*, Second Edition, Bloomberg, 2012.

Cormen, Thomas, Charles Leiserson, Ronald Rivest, and Clifford Stein, *Introduction to Algorithms*, 3rd Edition, MIT, 2009.

de Freitas, Nando, Machine Learning and Data Mining, University of British Columbia, video lectures.
`http://www.cs.ubc.ca/~nando/340-2012/`

Domingos, Pedro, *The Master Algorithm: How the Quest for the Ultimate Learning Machine Will Remake Our World*, Basic Books, 2015.

Downey, Allen, *Think Bayes*, O'Reilly, 2013.

—, *Think Python*, O'Reilly, 2012.

—, *Think Stats*, O'Reilly, 2011.

Easley, David, and Jon Kleinberg, *Networks, Crowds, and Markets*, Cambridge, 2010.

Fisher, Len, *The Perfect Swarm: The Science of Complexity in Everyday Life*, Basic, 2009.

Flach, Peter, *Machine Learning: The Art and Science of Algorithms that Make Sense of Data*, Cambridge, 2012.

Foreman, John, *Data Smart: Using Data Science to Transform Information into Insight*, Wiley, 2013.

Garreta, Raul, and Guillermo Moncechi, *Learning scikit-learn: Machine Learning in Python*, Packt, 2013.

Gigerenzer, Gerd, *Calculated Risks: How to Know When Numbers Deceive You*, Simon & Schuster, 2003.

Gutierrez-Osuna, Ricardo, Texas A&M University, *Lecture 13: Validation*.
`http://research.cs.tamu.edu/prism/lectures/iss/iss_ll3.pdf`

Haigh, John, *Taking Chances: Winning with Probability*, Oxford, 2003.

Harrington, Peter, *Machine Learning in Action*, Manning, 2012.

Hastie, Trevor, Robert Tibshirani, and Jerome Friedman, *The Elements of Statistical Learning: Data Mining, Inference, and Prediction*, Second Edition, Springer, 2011.

Hetland, Magnus Lie, *Python Algorithms: Mastering Basic Algorithms in the Python Language*, Second Edition, Apress - Springer, 2014.

Hubbard, Douglas, *How to Measure Anything: Finding the Value of Intangibles in Business*, Wiley, 2014.

Japkowicz, Nathalie, and Mohak Shah, *Evaluating Learning Algorithms: A Classification Perspective*, Cambridge, 2011.

Koller, Daphne, and Nir Friedman, *Probabilistic Graphical Models: Principles and Techniques*, MIT, 2009.

—, *Probabilistic Graphical Models*, Stanford University, Coursera online course.
`https://www.coursera.org/course/pgm`

Kruschke, John, *Doing Bayesian Analysis, Second Edition*, Academic Press, 2014.

Marsland, Stephen, *Machine Learning: An Algorithm Perspective*, CRC, 2009.

Mauboussin, Michael, *More Than You Know: Finding Financial Wisdom in Unconventional Places*, Columbia, 2007.

—, *The Success Equation: Untangling Skill and Luck in Business, Sports, and Investing*, Harvard, 2012.

McGrayne, Sharon Bertsch, *The Theory that Would Not Die: How Bayes Rule Cracked the Enigma Code, Hunted Down Russian Submarines, and Emerged Triumphant from Two Centuries of Controversy*, Yale, 2011.

McKinney, Wes, *Python for Data Analysis: Data Wrangling with Pandas, NumPy, and iPython*, O'Reilly, 2012.

Miller, Thomas, *Modeling Techniques in Predictive Analytics: Business Problems and Solutions with R*, Pearson, 2013.

Miner, Gary, Robert Nisbet, and John Elder, *Handbook of Statistical Analysis and Data Mining Applications*, Academic Press, 2009.

Moore, Andrew, Carnegie Mellon University, *Cross-validation for detecting and preventing overfitting.*
`https://www.autonlab.org/tutorials/overfit10.pdf`

Murphy, Kevin, *Machine Learning: A Probabilistic Perspective*, MIT Press, 2012.

Ng, Andrew, *Machine Learning*, Stanford University Open Course.
`http://openclassroom.stanford.edu/MainFolder/`
`CoursePage.php?course=MachineLearning`

Nisbet, Robert, John Elder, and Gary Miner, *Handbook of Statistical Analysis and Data Mining Applications*, Academic Press, 2009.

Pearl, Judea, *Causality: Models, Reasoning, and Inference*, Second Edition, Cambridge, 2009.

Peta, Joe, *Trading Bases: How a Wall Street Trader Made a Fortune Betting on Baseball*, New American Library, 2013.

Pratt, John, Howard Raiffa, and Robert Schlaifer, *Introduction to Statistical Decision Theory*, MIT, 1995.

Provost, Foster, and Tom Fawcett, *Data Science for Business: What You Need to Know About Data Mining and Data-Analytic Thinking*, O'Reilly, 2013.

Pyle, Dorian, *Data Preparation for Data Mining*, Morgan Kaufmann, 1999.

Raschka, Sebastian, *Python Machine Learning*, Packt, 2015.

—, *Terms in Data Science Defined in One Paragraph*, 2014,
https://github.com/rasbt/pattern_classification/blob/
master/resources/data_glossary.md

Rhoades, Russell, *Trading VIX Derivatives: Trading and Hedging
Strategies Using VIX Futures, Options, and Exchange Traded
Notes*, Wiley, 2011.

Richert, Willi, and Luis Pedro Coelho, *Building Machine Learning
Systems with Python*, Packt, 2013.

Russell, Stuart, and Peter Norvig, *Artificial Intelligence: A Modern
Approach*, Pearson, 2010.

Schapire, Robert, and Yoav Freund, *Boosting: Foundations and
Algorithms*, MIT, 2014.

Schutt, Rachell, and Cathy O'Neill, *Doing Data Science: Straight Talk
from the Frontline*, O'Reilly, 2014.

Sedgewick, Robert, and Kevin Wayne, *Algorithms*, 4th Edition,
Addison-Wesley, 2011.

Segaran, Toby, *Programming Collective Intelligence: Building Smart Web
2.0 Applications*, O'Reilly, 2007.

Siegel, Eric, and Thomas Davenport, *Predictive Analytics: The Power to
Predict Who Will Click, Buy, Lie, or Die*, Wiley, 2013.

Silver, Nate, *The Signal and the Noise: Why So Many Predictions Fail -
But Some Don't*,Penguin, 2012.

Steiner, Christopher, *Automate This: How Algorithms Came to Rule Our
World*, Portfolio / Penguin, 2012.

Stone, James, *Bayes Rule: A Tutorial Introduction to Bayesian Analysis*,
Sebtel, 2013.

Surowiecki, James, *The Wisdom of Crowds*, Random House, 2004.

Tan, Pang-Ning, Michael Steinbach, and Vipin Kumar, *Introduction to
Data Mining*, Pearson, 2005.

Tetlock, Philip, and Dan Gardner, *Superforecasting: The Art and Science
of Prediction*, Crown, 2015.

Vorhies, William, CRISP-DM—A Standard Methodology to Ensure a
Good Outcome.
http://www.datasciencecentral.com/profiles/blogs/
crisp-dm-a-standard-methodology-to-ensure-a-good-
outcome

Watts, Duncan, *Everything is Obvious: How Common Sense Fails Us*,
Crown, 2011.

Weisberg, Herbert, *Willful Ignorance: The Mismeasure of Uncertainty*, Wiley, 2014.

Wilson, Greg, et al, *Best Practices for Scientific Computing*, Cornell University, 2012.
http://arxiv.org/pdf/1210.0530v4.pdf

Winston, Patrick, *Artificial Intelligence*, MIT Open Courseware.
http://ocw.mit.edu/courses/electrical-engineering-and-computer-science/6-034-artificial-intelligence-fall-2010/

Witten, Ian, Eibe Frank, and Mark Hall, *Data Mining: Practical Machine Learning Tools and Techniques*, Third Edition, Morgan Kaufmann, 2011.

Index

Modeling Trading System Performance

Published in 2011

An introduction to Monte Carlo simulation.

Includes a free add-in for Excel that implements the procedures described in the *Foundations* book to compute risk, safe-f, and profit potential.

Learn more about the *Modeling* book, read the table of contents, some free full chapters, and the index on the book's own website:

www.ModelingTradingSystemPerformance.com

Or on Amazon, where you can use the look inside feature to read more and order your own copy:

https://www.amazon.com/dp/0979183820/

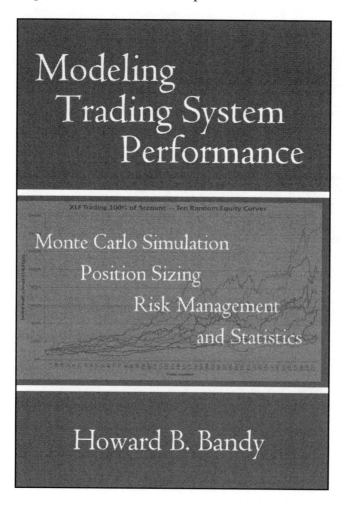

Mean Reversion Trading Systems

Published in 2013

Practical Methods for Swing Trading

Explanation of transformations.

Derivation of techniques to relax the restriction that lookback periods for the RSI indicator be an integer number of days.

Fully disclosed trading systems that trade frequently, trade accurately, and hold a few days.

Learn more about the *Mean Reversion* book, read the table of contents, some free full chapters, and the index on the book's own website:

www.MeanReversionTradingSystems.com

Or on Amazon, where you can use the look inside feature to read more and order your own copy:

https://www.amazon.com/dp/0979183847/

Quantitative Technical Analysis

Published in 2015

An integrated approach to trading system development and trading management.

Deeper discussion of risk, dynamic position sizing, and profit potential than in the *Foundations* book.

Includes an introduction to machine learning for trading using Python.

Learn more about the *QTA* book, read the table of contents, some free full chapters, and the index on the book's own website:

www.QuantitativeTechnicalAnalysis.com

Or on Amazon, where you can use the look inside feature to read more and order your own copy:

https://www.amazon.com/dp/0979183855/

18924895R00096

Printed in Poland
by Amazon Fulfillment
Poland Sp. z o.o., Wrocław